BIRTHING THE FIRE IN YOUR BELLY

ROSALIND GREEN

BIRTHING THE FIRE IN YOUR BELLY

It's Finally Time For You to PUSH and Deliver

◆◆◆◆◆◆◆◆◆◆◆◆◆◆◆◆

ROSALIND GREEN

Faith and Works Publishing

Copyright © 2016 Faith and Works 360°

All rights reserved. No portion of this publication may be reproduced, distributed, stored in a retrieval system, or transmitted in any form or by any means without prior written permission of the publisher.

Faith and Works Publishing
340 S. Lemon Avenue
Suite #5414
Walnut, CA 91789

Printed in the United States of America

ISBN-13: 978-0692476062 (Rosalind Green) ISBN-10:0692476067

Book Design by Faith and Works Publishing

To find out more about Rosalind Green visit: www.rosalindgreen.net

DEDICATION

◆◆◆◆◆◆◆◆◆◆◆◆◆

I dedicate this book to the most beautiful rose in the world, my mom, Rosetta Peppers, and the best big brother ever, Tyrone Peppers.

Mom, you taught me everything I know about giving back. It's because of you that this, my first book, has finally been written. You birthed me from your belly first and without even knowing, you inspired me to birth the fire in my own belly.

Our last years together were some of the most important, cherished years of my entire life. Thank you for that very special time and for the perfect example of a lady that you always were.

I love and miss you more than words could ever say or write.

Ert, I don't even have words. You have been there for me my whole life. You never got to read my book, but I know that you are proud of your little sis.

Thank you for just being available and always looking out, no matter what. I love you and wish you were here. I know you and mom are living it up in heaven.

ROSALIND GREEN

CONTENTS

	Foreword	9
	Acknowledgments	13
	Author's Note	15
	Introduction	17
1	Brick Walls CAN Be Knocked Down	21
2	What In The World Am I Doing Here?	31
3	God, You're Not Talking to Me… Are You?	43
4	Wait! What About Timing? Am I Ready for This?	51
5	Drowning Out the Noises In My Head	63
6	Should I Really Tell My Story?	77
7	They'll Call You Strange, But Be Uniquely You	89
8	No More Soft Talk… It's Time To Man-up (Woman Up)	97
9	You Do Have the Solution to Someone's Problem	105
10	Are You Using the F-I-R-E Formula?	115
11	Money is the Root of All Evil. Who Told You That Lie?	127
12	Let's Get Crystal Clear On the Vision	137
13	Managing The Many Facets of Your New Life	145
14	Oh No! Not Another Braxton-Hicks	161
15	Ready for the Delivery Table	169
16	Let's Go For the Final Push	177
17	You've Gotta Keep Fanning The Flame	187

FOREWORD

✦✦✦✦✦✦✦✦✦✦✦✦✦

Purpose and Destiny. Two words that we hear often, but are rarely defined. It all boils down to the understanding of exactly why you were birthed into this world, what you were intended to do, and who you are destined to be. The definition of purpose is "the reason why something is done or created," or why something exists; while destiny is said to be a predetermined course of events that are already determined to take place.

For many of us, when we find our purpose, our pre-determined destiny will be realized. When we don't find our purpose, we experience an irresistible power or urge that continually nudges us asking, "Who am I, why am I here, and what on earth am I supposed to be doing?"

I'd like you to know that you've just picked up **THE** book, written by **THE** author, who is superbly equipped and not only that, **ROSALIND GREEN** knows how to help passionately, you discover exactly what it is you are "called" to do, here on this earth! **ROSALIND GREEN** innately and intricately knows how to help you locate and pull out that very **"THING"** that has been assigned to you; to **DO** and **BE**!

I'm not speaking just from a voice of someone who has read her book and has been honored to write the foreword. I speak from a place of one who has taken her awesome courses on more than one occasion, and has now launched into a business that was stagnant, yet burning in my very own belly!

Over a year ago, I was blessed to birth my own business. I enjoyed my work more than anything else I'd done, but I did not receive adequate compensation. Most recently, **ROSALIND GREEN** pulled a best-selling book out of me, when I didn't even realize I had one sitting on the back burner just waiting to come through the birth canal and make its debut in the world!

In the day and time in which we now live, there is so much information available to us. There are self-help books, and a wealth of information on the superhighway called the Internet; in fact, you can look up or "Google" just about anything for which you need an answer. However, now and then there is one that surfaces from seemingly a place of obscurity and presents to us a solution that includes a formula, by which we can go from where we are to where we're supposed to be. *"Birthing the Fire in Your Belly,"* has found me, and many of you who will dare to read, right where you are. Not only may it find you right where you are, but it will also help you to get to where you have to go.

If you're an entrepreneur, a business owner, have a vision, or thinking about what you are going to do with your life, this book will help you get there. When you follow the steps that are perfectly laid out, you will be propelled right into your destiny.

"Birthing The Fire in Your Belly," is thought provoking, game-changing, yet easy to read. This book is written, in a casual, informative style, and will assist you

with that dream, that vision, that goal, that is inside of you. **ROSALIND GREEN** can help you get it from out of your heart, head, and spirit, into manifestation. I encourage you to buy not just one copy, but to get copies for others. We all need to birth our dreams and visions!

Be challenged, motivated, inspired and encouraged! No matter what has or hasn't worked for you in the past, know that this book will catapult you into places you've never been!

Dr. Beverly Crockett, Entrepreneur
CEO/Founder, Executive Business Writing

ACKNOWLEDGMENTS

◆◆◆◆◆◆◆◆◆◆◆◆◆

To my husband, Ronnie, thank you for being so patient. There were many hours that I sat at the computer not stopping for dinner and staying up to wee hours of the morning. Writing this book was a long road but you, as always, have been my rock and I love and appreciate you for that more than words could ever say.

To my daughter, LaTrisa, my only child; you've seen me through almost every bit of my journey—the good, the bad, the ugly and then some. You've laughed with me, cried with me, been silly in the stores so people would know I was your mom, and have become my closest friend (outside of Pop-pop). ☺ You've developed into a beautiful young woman, and I wouldn't trade any of our times together for the world.

To Ashlee, Brandon, and Caelin, the best grandkids in the world... you've always held a special place in my heart. I love the fact that you've been open to allowing me to interject my thoughts and ideas into your lives (even when you didn't want to hear it). I'm so proud of all three of you.

To my itty-bitty great-grands, Noah, Aria, and A.J.—one day you'll be old enough to read this book, and it's my prayer that you'll always know that from day one, Grammie always believed that you would do great things in life. You mean the world to me.

To my uncle and aunt, Rev. Laddie and Mrs. Emma B. Peppers. You are two of the most upstanding people I have ever had the privilege to know. Whenever I think of perfect love, a perfect couple, and true lovers of God, I think of you. Thank you for all the years of love. I still have a long way to go, but I wouldn't be who I am today without all of the things you instilled in me as a child.

Thank you to my church family for always encouraging me to be all that God has called me to be. Your prayers and belief in what's on the inside of me will never be forgotten.

To San, my "bossy bestie"... girl, what can I say. You are my ride or die and always will be. Thanks for all of your prayers, encouragement, long talks, and more.

And for those who made my life a little tough at times, from childhood until it just didn't matter anymore, I acknowledge you because, without you, my story and my journey would be a little different and this book might never have been written.

And last, but certainly not least... to God be the glory for the things that He has done and is continuing to do every day!

AUTHOR'S NOTE

♦♦♦♦♦♦♦♦♦♦♦♦♦♦♦

Because you've chosen to pick up this book, I would like to give you a small token of appreciation that I believe will help you birth the fire in your belly.

As you read through these pages, you'll come to a point where you realize that you're ready to take the next step in your journey, whatever it might be, and I'd like to help you start the process.

You'll understand that being in action is important and necessary in walking toward your destiny, but you also need to know what steps to take. My biggest thrill is to help you launch your mission into the world, and I couldn't be happier than to have an opportunity to play a small part in that.

As you read this book, I don't want just to inspire or motivate you. I also want to give you the processes to do something about showing up the way you were intended.

Once you have read the book, I encourage you to contact me for a personal FREE consultation to help you birth the fire that's brewing in your belly right now. To receive your gift, visit the following website:

www.birthingthefirechallenge.com

INTRODUCTION

◆◆◆◆◆◆◆◆◆◆◆◆◆

I wonder sometimes what it is that keeps most of us living in a state of discontent, frustration, and still looking for what we're supposed to be doing with our lives.

We know that we have something deep inside our gut that says, this is what you were born for. We aren't content with the "same way, same time, same place" mentality, but for some reason trying to break out of it seems next to impossible.

We go to our jobs, and we hate the fact that we don't seem to have a choice. We go to our networking events and it's always the same people, saying and doing the same thing. We go to our churches and wonder why nothing has changed for the last ten years. Not that there's anything wrong with any of this, but then the question becomes… "where do I fit into the scheme of all of this beyond keeping the company going, or keeping the church going, or showing up to the event because I'm expected to."

There is nothing worse than having purpose buried so deep inside your belly that you almost forget that it exists.

Who have you become? Who's life are you living and what purpose are you fulfilling? These unanswered questions are some of the most common among people today. Everybody knows that there has got to be something more, but what does it mean for me and how do I find it?

This book was written for those who know that there is something brewing within their very soul that is keeping you from being comfortable with the "business as usual" way of thinking. You aren't satisfied with the status quo. You know that there is purpose deep inside you and you are ready to release it into the world.

The greatest part about all of this is that you are seeking answers. You've come to the place where you are no longer content to sit on the sidelines waiting for destiny to fall in your lap. You're ready to go after it. Good for you!

You might be wondering how I know this about you. Well, let's say that it takes a special kind of person to pick up and actually read books like this. It's not every day that we run into people who want to go beyond normalcy. I know about you because that was once me.

I do realize that some people read books for shear entertainment. Nothing wrong with that at all, but my guess is that that's not you. My belief about you is that you are ready to discover the when, what, and how of your life. You've thought about things, prayed about some stuff, sought solutions, and you won't stop until you're well on your way to finding answers.

Again... good for you. I love meeting people who have not only sight, but also vision. And, even though I may not know you personally right now, I believe that I know who you are because again, you're a lot like me.

You're a person of hope who realizes that living a life fulfilled doesn't have to be a pipe dream, but can be your reality. You're a person who is open to gaining the knowledge and understanding you need to take your life into your next season.

You know that transformation for you is not only

possible, but can be tangible, is long overdue and you're ready for it. Again, good on you. You've done a good thing by picking up this book. I encourage you to read every page. Don't skip the introduction just because it's not one of the main chapters. Every part of this book has significance that I don't want you to miss.

I've made sure that this book is written with straight talk and for "easy reading." I want you to have a clear understanding that it is your time and your dreams don't have to continue to be squashed and buried. If you've buried them already, it's time to dig them up.

It's my hope that as you read this book, the fire that's been simmering in your belly… (the vision, purpose, passion, destiny…) will be rekindled and turn into a blaze that will be hard for you to contain.

If you've lost your confidence, it's time to get it back. If you've been told that it's not your time and years have gone by (and it's still not your time), it's time to revisit what you've set aside and redeem the time that is ahead.

It's time for you to live a life that you love. As I like to put it, love what you do what you love. It's possible. It's also possible that you can allow the "real you" to come out of hiding and stop covering up all of those gifts, talents, dreams and aspirations that you know exist inside you.

You may have had days, weeks, months… heck, even years that have gone by since you thought about some of those things that were once real plans of yours. I get it. Life happens and sometimes those plans just don't seem to fit within the scope of our lives any more. I also realize that sometimes it has been our own decision to let some of those things go. I get that too.

How about now you go back and remind yourself of why you really wanted to do some of those things to begin with.

At this point, you are about to go on a journey. Not a deep one and not one that will have you in some weird mind space. This journey is one that will cause those dead fires to start burning in you once again. You may think that they're just ashes right now, but all we need to do is reignite them with a new wick and some fresh oil and they're back to burning again.

I know you want that and I want that for you. So let's get ready. If you've had some unspoken desires pinned up in your heart, it's time to speak them out and let them loose.

And whatever you do, don't ever think that it's too late. It's never too late. Some things may be a little different now than they once were. That's okay, too. We'll pick up right where you are now and move forward from here.

As you read through these pages, I want you to do some self-examination on where you are now and where you want to be. Keep your mind on the latter and don't let anything or anyone distract you from doing all you can to bring that vision into full fruition.

Again, let me say how proud I am of you and how excited I am for you. You are now about to be transformed, so get ready.

CHAPTER 1

♦ ♦ ♦ ♦ ♦ ♦ ♦ ♦ ♦ ♦

BRICK WALLS *CAN* BE KNOCKED DOWN

(The chapter that almost didn't make it in the book)

> *"Don't let that 'fake it 'til you make it' trick come back to bite you. It's not for everyone..."*

For starters, let me explain that this book is for anyone who has vision and purpose but for some reason it's been sitting on the shelf, and you're not sure how to take it down and blow the dust off. That includes gifts, talents, abilities and more.

Who can benefit from reading this book? Authors, speakers, entrepreneurs, ministry leaders, Believers, non-believers, teachers, lawyers, chefs, florists, parents, teens, I could go on. And believe it or not, this goes completely against the grain of what I share when it comes to knowing who the people are that need to hear your voice.

I just want you to know, that it doesn't matter what your

walk of life might be right now. There's something (or more like someone) calling out to you or you wouldn't be reading this book.

You may not even be entirely sure what that tug is all about. It's okay; you're not alone. Just keep reading. I believe your answers are very, very close now.

Now that you have a slightly better idea of what this is really about, let me take this opportunity for a small "side-step" before we get into this journey.

How odd it is that the section you're reading right now at the beginning of this book, was written ninety days after I thought the book was finished. There's a reason.

The truth is, if you have something to say or something to do that needs to go beyond the walls of your mind, this book is for you.

All through this book, I talk to you about things like...

1) Keep pushing through even though you're feeling fearful.

2) Don't let anything or anybody stop you from doing what you're called to do.

3) Don't let the lies of your past stop you from moving forward.

I talk about how your personal story shouldn't stop you but should move you deeper into your journey. I talk about knowing who you are, what you're purposed to do in the world and how to go about doing it.

Then why did I (the person who's writing about birthing this great fire) get stuck right when it was time to push the "publish" button... just when it was time to begin my own birthing process?

I came to realize that I needed to write this chapter not only for myself, but for somebody who needs to read it because it's exactly where you are right now. It's all part of the final phase of the delivery process which will make a lot more sense once you've read the rest of the book.

The reality is, I couldn't have completed this book without having lived through what I'm about to share with you. Don't worry; I'll keep it light (well, sort of).

As you read, you'll come across a mention of my mom passing away, but I may not have said that it happened just a couple of months before I started to write this book.

Mom was 92 years young, a good Christian woman, and she was ready to go to her home in heaven. I remember just a few days before her passing how she sang praises and prayed for everyone who was special to her. She thanked the people who had been so caring and kind to her during the two years she came to live with me—just before her passing. She knew it was her time, and she was ready. She was in a good place— a much better place than I was about the whole thing.

After everything was over, at least all of the busy things that you have to go through when a loved one passes on, I knew that writing this book was next on my bucket list. It's something I had promised my mom that I would do.

Initially, I'd set out to write a book about my mom and me. It was going to be about how we started life with me being her baby and how we ended with her being mine. But whenever I would sit to write, I couldn't get past a paragraph or two without turning into a blubbering I don't know what.

So, I decided to set that book aside and write the one that she and I had talked about instead. You're reading it right now.

It's all good now, but somewhere along the way, all of the pinned up emotions that I'd been experiencing behind her death and many things that happened afterward got shoved under a rug. I tried with everything I had to continue going on as usual. After all, I'm a strong Christian woman, too. I have faith in God, and I know that Mom's in a better place. I also know that she was ready to go... at least at the very end. So it's okay for me to move on and live my life—right? Of course, it is.

Then why did everything in me shut down right at the end of a workshop I was teaching about how to write and publish your first book. Ironic, right? Yes... I took people on this book-writing journey with me. I wanted to write this book to honor my mother, and I wanted to do it by holding a workshop with a small group of writers who also wanted to become published authors. I was going to do Mom proud.

But as soon as we got to the last session, the one where you actually push the button and send your book to the printer, I crashed. That fire I was trying to birth couldn't even muster up a simmering spark.

At that point, everything that was familiar to me, the things I did for fun and work, all of my social media, coaching, everything... all went by the wayside in one big thunk! I didn't plan it, and I didn't see it coming. It was like an entire part of my life just vanished somewhere into thin air and I wasn't interested in trying to find where it went.

I didn't feel that I was running from anything. All I knew was I just didn't want to do or deal with anything extra. I would eat, go to the office to notarize documents for an attorney twice a week, go to church on Sunday and wear my fake smile as though I was just fine, and sleep. That was it. I wasn't mad at God, and I didn't feel any anger towards any person. I didn't blame anyone and all was well... well, not really.

The oddest thing about all of this was that my "shut-down" didn't happen until five months after mom died. My birthday triggered it all. I was sitting at my desk in my home office. I was in the process of putting the finishing touches on my book; then it hit me.

This birthday was the very first of my entire life that my mom was not here. I know. That's probably pretty petty because I'm well aware that people have these types of losses every day. But I'd never lost a mother before and didn't know what to expect. I hit a brick wall, and it took me out for the count—5 months AFTER she'd passed on.

Now mind you... you'll read later that there were many birthdays where my mom wasn't physically with me. True, there were years where our relationship was almost nonexistent, but she was still where I could get that call or think about some of the great times we'd shared together. This time, I couldn't pick up the phone and a void that I'd never felt before came from nowhere and wiped me out. I'd never missed my mom more in my life than I did this day.

The funny part—I didn't even realize that I'd cut everything off... shut everything down. It just happened little by little until everything was still. No noise in my head, no movement in my heart, just a numb, plastic smile that pretended that all was well.

You might wonder, what this has to do with birthing a dream, a vision or that fire. Well, I'll tell you.

Sometimes in life things happen that we have absolutely no control over. Often those things are not good, but they can be very common—like a person dying when they're in their 90's. That's normal and is expected. Well, it may be normal, but losing my mom certainly wasn't my normal.

When something happens in your life that is not normal for you, your subconscious mind tries to find the best way possible to make it normal. We all have different ways of responding to things that are hard for us.

Some people take to drugs and drinking. Some may party a little too hard. Some curse God, and some ignore and suppress it trying to pretend that life goes on as usual because people expect us to—because of who we are (or who they perceive us to be).

So, what was so hard, so intense, that I couldn't function? Was it guilt that I wasn't there for her more in some of her later years? Was it anger that she wasn't there for me in some of my earlier years? Was it because I felt cheated that when I finally got her to myself, she was gone after just two short years? I could go on, but you get the picture.

I had a lot of things brewing in my heart and soul, and all of those things contributed to my shutdown. What I probably should have had was a meltdown so I could at least get it out and get it over with. I never questioned God. Instead, I just cut off what I could without it being noticed (so I thought). Now... back to what this has to do with birthing my own fire.

One tiny part of my dream, part of the fire that I needed to birth myself, was to write this book. Just when it was time for me make that final push, I chose to stop the contractions and hop off of the delivery table. Here's the kicker. If you've ever had a baby, or you've been in the delivery room when someone else was about to deliver, you know that just because you don't feel like pushing anymore doesn't stop the contractions from coming. If you stop pushing, it just delays the delivery. Sometimes, the doctors will even give you something to keep the contractions coming with little effort on your part. Either way, those contractions are not going to stop just because you want to quit.

This is the time where you have to figure out how to work through those delivery pains or real-life hindrances, whatever they might be, and get that baby out! You have a moral obligation to the baby that you're carrying; the fire you're trying to birth. It's now time to give it a chance to take that first breath and live, but it first has to be born.

And know especially, that if what you're birthing has anything at all to do with what God has assigned and appointed you to, there will be obstacles— and don't think that they will always be from "the devil." Sometimes those forces are coming from right inside your very soul.

Common occurrences like getting laid off from a job, going through bankruptcy or foreclosure, mental and physical abuse, you name it... can contribute to you hitting that brick wall.

I'd like to tell you that if that happens, just act like it didn't and go ahead and do what you started out to do. But because I believe in being transparent and authentic, I'm not going to tell you that. Why not? I can't tell you that with a clear conscience because that's not what happened for me.

In this book, you'll find things that I can attest to personally, not just something I read about or heard talked about by someone else. I will tell you that ignoring your issues and treating them as though they don't exist will only prolong your delivery and your time to recover.

I'd also like to say to those who are Believers that because of our faith, it's rare that we are willing to admit that our prayers didn't seem to work. Can we be real? Prayer is enough but, brick walls will come, and sometimes it takes more than you chipping away at them by yourself.

Get those who know how to pray to chip with you. And just like those brick walls are formed, they can be broken down with just a little consistent effort.

So, what do I suggest? You still have to deliver this fire in your belly. If a brick wall of any sort has you stuck, get a hammer and just start chipping away one small rock at a time. Yes, I did say one little piece.

Sometimes you won't be able to chisel a whole brick all at once. It's okay. Just keep chucking the little pieces. Some days, the chisel will be so heavy you may not even feel like picking it up. It's okay. Rest, but keep it in plain view. Don't put it away.

When you keep the chisel in clear view, you can't help but see it every day. It will stare you in the face and compel you to pick it up and start chipping at your brick wall again. Some days you'll be strong enough to knock down ten bricks at a time. However it comes, just keep chipping. Then, one day it happens. You look up, and there is only a tiny powder residue where that brick wall once stood so high.

Finding that powdery residue happened to me just a few days before I wrote this final section, which again, was written three months after I thought I had finished the book. So what happened?

Somewhere way down in the gut of my spirit, I saw that wall, and I looked at that chisel. I went and got a bigger, heavier hammer. I started swinging at that wall... through tears, through anger, through fear, through love, through hurt and all of the mortar that had been holding that ugly wall together.

I first forgave myself, then I forgave and prayed for others that I felt I needed to forgive. I cried some more, and I kept swinging. I prayed out loud, and I kept swinging. Then I was exhausted and put the hammer down, and I finally said it with my mouth. God, I'm tired. I'm done. I can't carry it anymore. It's yours.

Even though I never actually hit a physical wall and there was no real hammer in my hand, it was all too real in my gut and so was my release.

Once I stopped swinging,... (again in my spirit) I felt peace. I knew that from that point on, all was well; for real this time. No more wearing fake and phony smiles feeling like I needed to pretend. No more feeling the need to "represent" that "minister of the gospel" who is so "strong in the Lord" and has no issues. It was finally over. This drama was over. In my spirit, I saw the little bitty pile of dust where the wall once stood and all of a sudden I heard it.

Wah.... Wah.... Wah... The baby was out. Wow... Breaking through that brick wall was part of my final stages of labor and birthing. Who knew? Okay, I'm good now. I look a hot mess, but this baby is beautiful and so well worth the entire delivery process.

My immediate response when I truly felt at peace was "God, thank you for allowing me to carry and deliver this book. I didn't climb over the wall; I didn't go through or around it, but you allowed me to break down this seemingly impossible hurdle. Thank you for my release and right now—as this baby is finally born—I dedicate it back to you."

This book is birthed out of a desire to completely surrender to the will of God for my own life. It is my prayer that it will help you tear down walls of disappointment, discouragement, fear, doubt and just plain not knowing fully what is the call and purpose that God has for your life.

Since this book has fallen into your hands, I can only believe that you are on the verge of wanting to give birth to the fire in your own belly. Let this book bring you to the delivery table and be that strength that gives you the urge to go for that final push. I want you to push until you are walking in your God-appointed calling and purpose. God, this book is yours. Bless it and do with it as you will.

Now, on to the beginning of this journey.

CHAPTER TWO

◆ ◆ ◆ ◆ ◆ ◆ ◆ ◆ ◆ ◆

WHAT IN THE WORLD AM I DOING HERE?

"Wait, this is not my life. This belongs to somebody else. Can the real me please stand up?"

My guess is that you picked up this book because you know without a shadow of a doubt that you've been called to do something great in the world. Not great for making people look at you as someone super special, but great in how super special you're able to help transform someone else's life.

I've been there, and I know that feeling all too well.

I remember sitting in my office on a particularly rainy day... when a shift happened and my whole world changed. I walked into the office and put down my briefcase. I didn't even bother to turn on the light. I sat there in the quiet, just listening to the rain. Usually, as soon as I come into the office, I would turn on some soft music in the background and pop on the lights, but not today. Today, something was different. No lights, no music, just me behind this big, oversized desk in this huge oversized office.

The only light coming through was from the sun that had miraculously appeared in the middle of the dark rain cloud. It was shining pretty bright from my beautiful floor to ceiling windows that covered a whole wall.

Another common ritual of mine was to go straight to the bathroom (yes, a private bathroom right inside my office), to make sure that my makeup was still flawless, and that every hair of my slicked back bun was still in place before starting my day. Oh yes, and that my perfectly pressed, pin-striped, pencil-skirted suit was still wrinkle-free after having to put a seat belt over it as I drove in. I did none of that today.

I sat at my desk and just looked around. I looked at the walls of bookcases filled with legal books and files. There were books about being a good leader, books about how to manage staff in the corporate space so that they would willingly do what you wanted or needed them to do. I remember my thoughts as I stared at the books in the bookcases on top of the credenza behind my big huge desk.

Everything looked huge today. The shelves on my credenza were stuffed with more books about all kinds of things that, at this time, for me, I had absolutely no interest.

I wasn't sure what was happening with me today. All I know was it didn't feel good. I'd had enough sleep the night before, and I wasn't sad, depressed or ungrateful. I knew that there were probably millions of people in the world who would LOVE to have my life right now.

But today my thoughts were different. "How did I get

here? Why am I feeling so empty? Can I just get up and leave and never come back?" I'd felt this before but this time, it wasn't just a feeling. I wasn't even aware, but something radical was happening on my insides that would cause me to make a another one of those shifts that would completely change my life.

This shift was drawing me away from what I'd been doing for years out of necessity and familiarity. It was drawing me to what I was put on this earth to do, and it had nothing to do with anything that was familiar.

There was almost an inner ache that I couldn't squash, and it was heavy. I was in labor and didn't know it. I wasn't sure why, but I think I was about to feel a tear well up in my eyes when the phone rang and almost startled me.

Just that fast, I was back in the trenches... doing what I'd always done. Well... so much for trying to figure this one out today. Life is calling, and I have to go. On with the lights and on to my beautiful, personally decorated bathroom to check for flaws before I meet with one of the judicial officers of the court. Time to put out another fire that I had nothing to do with starting. For now, it's who I am in the world, and this is what I do.

Who are you in the world?

I'm a strong believer that God didn't allow any of us to be born into this world just to take up more space and use more oxygen. I believe that we were all given dreams, aspirations, desires and more. And for many of us, those dreams define how we show up in the world and what we do with what we've been given. These dreams don't just define who we are in our homes with our families or on our jobs, but who we are in this great big world in which we live.

Have you ever thought about it?

When you are thinking your happiest, most fulfilling thoughts... who are you being at that very moment? Think beyond those moments when you're just having a great time playing with your kids. Go beyond those fun vacations and travels that you've been blessed to experience. Look deeper than the last fun outing, wedding, or party that you attended. When you dig deeper, how are you showing up? Can you grasp what I'm asking?

When you've helped someone in some way, whether through a conversation, a gift that you gave, a service that you offered... how did you feel? What are you doing when you get that overwhelming feeling of pure joy, satisfaction, and fulfillment? Who were you being at those moments? Not when you're trying, but when you're being.

I know that many of us have something that we're so passionate about that we could almost do it every day, and we wouldn't complain much if we never received any compensation in return.

Do you have that "thing"? It's that something that you know that when you share it with people it changes their lives. Do you have a gift that when you give it, it brings a smile to the face of the person on the receiving end as well as yours? That's the "thing" I'm talking about. Who are you being during those times when you are completely walking in just a small glimpse of the purpose you were put on this earth to fill? Just in case you aren't sure or have any doubt whatsoever, yes, there is a very special space in this world just for you to fill and no one else can take your place. No one.

Sometimes, discovering that space isn't easy, but let me

share a little secret with you. It's usually only difficult because most people don't believe that they have what it takes to actually walk in whatever that calling is. Let me explain.

What if you knew that there was a need for unique hair products specifically for African American women and that you were supposed to create them? And what if in the process, you became the first black female in your country to become a millionaire? Maybe everyone around you thought you were crazy when you first started talking about it, but you always believed that you could do it, so you did.

What if you had the gift of writing books and plays that would cause a whole culture to look at their lives and laugh, cry, or find hope that there is light at the end of a dark tunnel. What if you turned those plays into movies that you would direct and even give yourself leading roles to play? And let's think about the remote possibility that those movies would create jobs and make millions that would eventually become an entertainment empire; all of this after you'd been turned down time and time again?

What if you understood the financial struggle that many people live under. As a result, you had an unction to establish a successful business model where you could give ordinary people an extraordinary opportunity to start businesses of their own. And suppose that as a result, you were able to help tens of thousands save their families from financial ruin?

These are just a few examples of real people who had real dreams and a purpose that went far beyond themselves. They stared the possibilities of what could be right in the face. And while, no doubt, there were many around these real people who thought they were crazy to believe they could do the things they did, they still had the guts to move out in what they believed. As a result, their lives were forever changed and so were the lives of many others. What if you had that same tenacity to "feel the fear and do it anyway" or as I've also heard it put, "do it scared!"

When you begin to dig deep, you'll usually find that that "thing" that is deposited in you reaches much farther than what you (and most people) would dare expect. You think it's too big for you. Or, you think "that's a really good idea, and somebody should be doing that." Why not you?

To make big things happen, all it starts with is a dream, a purpose, a vision and a willingness to dig deep enough to figure it all out. First, you figure out what it is. Next, you figure out what it would take to make it happen. Then, you just do it

My bet is that you probably don't have to dig too deep or search that hard to get to the first step; that step of knowing that there's something out there calling you. Once you figure out who you are supposed to be in the world, the next step is to figure out what you need to do to begin the process of actually bringing it to fruition. And that part is up to you. You're the one with the "tug" so don't ignore it. It's there for a reason.

When Passion and Purpose Merge

In case you're not really sure about what your "thing" might be, here's a fun little exercise that we did at one of my workshops. If you do it too, I believe it will help you gain some clarity.

Picture this, (We closed our eyes, but you don't have to

because you're reading... that was for a chuckle.) You're being asked to go to a tropical island. It's beautiful. It has amazing waterfalls and scenic views everywhere you turn. You have a personal chef to prepare all of your meals and butlers who will handle all of the cleaning and daily household maintenance. Everything that you even think you need is already taken care of.

You're staying in the most adorable beach house with every amenity you could imagine, (or maybe a man cave just in case the "adorable" thing doesn't work for you.) You're told that you must stay on this island for at least 30 days and at the end of the 30 days, you will be given five million dollars to fund your dream. And it doesn't matter at all what that dream is. It might be one that seems really strange to some, but it's still your dream.

There's just one thing. You can't take anyone with you, so you'll be there alone. You can only take your clothes and three other items. The three items that you take must have something to do with how you'll put the millions of dollars to use. There is also a stipulation. Before you can collect the reward, there is something you absolutely must do.

While you're there, you must "do" something for a minimum of four hours during the day and two hours in the evenings. Every single day that you're there, you have to do this. If you miss even one day, you will forfeit the million dollar reward that comes at the end.

With clearness of mind, there are two simple questions you need to answer.

1. What three items in addition to your clothes and toiletries will you take to the island with you?

2. What will you do with them while you're there?

Take a minute to think about it and answer it for yourself before moving on.

Now... you've come to the end of your 30-day sabbatical, and they throw in something that you did not expect. It was all a hoax. There is no money at the end of this experiment. Yes, you got the 30 days on the island, and you were well taken care of. You had everything you needed. You had some time away from your norm, and you got some space to breathe.

So after you get over being angry because you got duped, you realize that all you've gotten from this little experience was a free vacation. You got time alone, and you had hours to spend doing something you (hopefully) loved. How do you feel about this?

Maybe you're angry about the deception, and rightfully so. No one likes to be deceived like that, but it's over now. How do you feel about that time you spent doing whatever you chose?

Do you feel that you totally wasted 30 days of your life hoping for something that was never going to be made available to you? Or, are you better for having had an opportunity to steal away and spend 30 days with something you love and are passionate about that could also potentially catapult you into your purpose?

Here's a secret. If you don't feel the second statement, you might need to keep digging for the three things you really should have taken because you haven't found that "thing" yet.

To whom much is given...

I really used to get tired of hearing people quote the scripture in Luke 12:48 that says "to whom much is given, much is required." In my opinion, it was a little unfair. My thoughts would usually be "you don't know that some of what I've been given resulted in me being hurt, sad, taking hard knocks, being miserable and feeling used and abused."

See, some of the stuff I was given, or should I say... most of it, I didn't ask for. Not only did I not ask for it, if I could have thrown it back, I would have done so without hesitation. Now I'm expected to just chalk it all up as an experience that I was given—for what? Was it for the sole purpose of helping someone else through their issues? What's right or fair about that? Nothing. What's right about using it to help others? Everything.

In most cases, unfortunately, we don't get to choose what we've been handed in life. We're born into the family, generation, and culture that we were supposed to be born into. In different phases of our lives, things happen that we just had no control over.

What we *can* choose is what we eventually do with what we've been handed. We can choose to eat too much food until we're sick and overweight, or we can choose to push the plate away and go to the gym so we'll look better and feel great.

We can choose to marry the first person who comes along and appears to be interested in us, or we can wait... and wait... and wait... (and wait some more) until the very best person that God has for us finally shows up. (Thank God I finally got it right!)

We can also decide to use the thing—the very thing that we've struggled with the most to help someone else who is still struggling. Again, we do have a choice in the matter.

When it comes to how we show up in the world, we can choose to ask God for clarity then act on it. We could also choose to look the other way because what He's telling us to do seems too complicated. Either way, it's ours to choose.

I often wonder how our lives would be if God hadn't been so gracious in giving us the right to choose. I think His choices would have been much better than the ones we sometimes make.

Many things are required of us, and I don't believe that most of them are forced on us against our will. Yes, sometimes people will force themselves (even inappropriately) on us, because of their physical strength or mental instability. And sometimes they may yell so loud that we can't hear our own inner voice crying out.

But when it comes to deciding what we do with those dreams we were given, more often than not, we are the ones who choose to allow them to die and fade away. In some instances, those passions become fleeting thoughts that get buried so deep we forget they ever existed.

However, have you ever thought that sometimes, those passions are there to draw out of us what needs to show up for the rest of the world?

There are times that we need a little extra "kick" to get us moving, but the best kick we can get is the one that comes from within our own souls. We have to "take responsibility for what we are responsible for." Did you get that?

When we're assigned to something specific, especially those things that can bring change to the world, we have a responsibility not just to ourselves, but also to all of those people who are supposed to be touched in some way because we "showed up" the way we were supposed to.

Keep in mind—we aren't given gifts and talents, wisdom and knowledge, or even certain life experiences just for ourselves. Everything you've lived through, once again, the good, the bad, and the ugly, has shown up in your life because of and in spite of. It's all a part of your story. It's your experience. So, don't look at these situations with that "oh well" or "whatever" mindset. Use them as a springboard to make a difference for someone who's living in the middle of it right now.

CHAPTER THREE

GOD, YOU'RE NOT TALKING TO ME... ARE YOU?

> *"This may not be your dream, but everybody has one... Seek the message inside yours."*

In case you aren't aware, God has many different ways of getting our attention. When we spend time with Him, sometimes His words to us are loud and clear. There are also those times that He speaks to us beautifully in our dreams to convey a message that we have somehow missed in our awakened hours.

I was talking to my friend, Sandi, the other day about a dream she'd had the night before. You know the one. We all have that one. If you haven't had yours yet, you will. This is a brief version of what she said.

"I was standing on a cliff overlooking this huge body of

water. There was someone standing next to me. I wasn't at all afraid of the person or of being on this high cliff. I was just taking it all in. I was also pregnant." Mind you... my friend already has grandchildren and is definitely not at a point in life where she'd ever consider having more children of her own. I had to chuckle a little at the thought of visualizing her pregnant, but asked her to go on.

She went on to tell of how there was a person standing next to her who suddenly pushed her off the cliff and into the body of water. The push was not done in a way to harm her and she wasn't afraid when she was pushed. She wasn't afraid while she was falling and she wasn't afraid when she landed in the water. There was also no fear of any harm coming to the "baby" she was carrying in her belly.

Her fear didn't come initially. It came when she realized that she was coming up out of that huge body of water that she had been looking over, and she couldn't swim. Mind you, she wasn't drowning or struggling in the water. I had to chuckle again. "You mean, you got scared once you were coming out and not when you first got pushed in?" "Very funny," she said, then we spent the next thirty minutes talking about it.

When I thought about it again later, I remembered how Peter walked on water with no fear until he realized that he was doing something that he wasn't supposed to naturally be able to do.

Because in her dream she was carrying a baby in her belly that we both knew didn't represent a human being, I decided to ask God about it and His answer prompted me to share it here because of what it meant.

My friend was standing on a cliff high above the ground which I knew meant that she had received a heightened level of understanding or awareness in a particular area of life. She'd be growing in her level of wisdom and knowledge.

When you are pregnant with a child, one thing that you must start learning about is how to be a mother. You learn how to nurture and care for the gift that you are carrying. As soon as you realize that you are carrying something, you want to position yourself to learn how to care for it properly. You want to make sure that you are receiving the proper nutrients to ensure that your baby is developing well.

The fact that my friend was standing at the edge of this cliff was an indication that she had been doing the right things to enlighten herself and heighten her awareness of how to care for this baby that she would soon birth. Her level of understanding had been elevated. I happened to know that she'd been doing a lot of studying, reading, and spending time in prayer and had been receiving many downloads of wisdom and knowledge surrounding a certain thing.

That brings us to you. You have this fire in your belly. Have you been preparing yourself to care for it properly? You may not know if it's a boy or a girl and his or her features haven't yet been revealed. You may not be clear if your baby will have you speaking, writing, teaching, or something else. You don't know completely what your baby will look like, but you know it will have traces of who you are. In actuality, you may not even have the baby bump, yet. But if you know without a doubt that you are pregnant, whether others can see it yet or not doesn't matter. You have to prepare yourself. Don't just assume that you'll automatically know what to do when it's time to deliver.

As Sandi was standing on the edge of that cliff, the view was beautiful to her. In her conscious life, she would never have dived into the water on her own because she knew that she couldn't swim. She needed the confidence that she would be okay if she just jumped in. Apparently, the person standing with her was attempting to talk her through it, but she wouldn't go voluntarily, so he gave her a little shove.

What I also know about my friend is that she is very gifted in a lot of areas. However, trying to get her out there to use those gifts is a whole other story. I recall one time when we were all in a room at my house just singing and worshipping. She was really touching heaven and we all got quiet and just listened. As soon as she realized that she was the only one singing, she stopped right in the middle of a long, beautiful note that she'd been holding.

Huh? What just happened? We all got snatched right back down to earth because she didn't have the confidence to keep going alone. She had no idea how beautiful it was.

It's a given that some of the things that we're called to do, we don't do alone. But let's be clear. If you are being led by God, you already know that you are not alone in the thing that you are about to birth even if, at times, it feels like it's just you. Understand that it's not at all about just you and your natural abilities. You are not alone in this.

At the same time, know that you'll need a midwife of sorts to help you bring your vision into the world. This is that person who is willing to stand with you, work with you, and be your personal cheer leader. Or perhaps they will be your coach or mentor who will give you that little "push" off the side of the cliff if you don't jump in when it's time.

While you may not need a cheering squad, you do need someone who believes in you and will assist you in areas where you can't go it alone. The best of the best have help. So should you. Your "midwife" is there make sure that you'll push when you need to and rest when it's necessary.

So, take a moment and think about it. Do you know who that person is who's standing with you? Right now, before it's time for you to deliver, is a good time to start thinking about who is on your team. Let them know that you'll need them to be on post when the time comes.

Usually, when we look ahead at what's to come, we have no fear. All we know is that we will soon be giving birth to a beautiful baby who will be making its way into this world soon. You aren't afraid to jump because you have no doubt that this fire has a purpose. You're actually excited about the possibilities, even though you may not know quite what to expect.

That's when the fear often comes. You'll be doing just fine then all of a sudden, you may start to experience the same fear that Sandi felt. She didn't experience fear when she went into the water. Fear came when she realized she was in something that she wasn't sure she could handle.

Guess what… If you're already pregnant, the journey has begun and it's no time to turn around. I suppose in a dream, anything can happen. However, if God is talking to you in yours, it's not likely that He'll let you reverse the reel and fly backwards to the cliff. You're already in the water and you're safe. Just like Peter wasn't supposed to be able to walk on water, Sandi wasn't supposed to be able to swim. But neither of them ended up there on their own strength and will.

By the way, peaceful water often signifies that you're in spiritual flow. That's why there was no initial fear. She was right where she needed to be when she was supposed to be there. Fear only happened when natural thoughts came in and interfered.

I don't know how big your vision is, but you'll hear me say this more than once. If you didn't have the capacity to carry it out, it wouldn't have been given to you. It doesn't matter that you've never done this before or that it's something you have little confidence in when it comes to your abilities to carry it out.

New mothers can read all of the books in the world about what it takes to be a good mother. In reality, it's not until she gives birth and brings the baby home that she knows what kind of mother she will actually be. My point... don't let the fear of the unknown keep you from jumping in the water.

Even though Sandi wasn't afraid when she was pushed, I'm sure she would have much preferred to jump in on her own so that she would have been better prepared. The truth is, as long as you are willing, whether you're ready or not, you will end up in the water. Sandi didn't drown and she was well aware of her surroundings. Know that you may come to some unfamiliar ground as you dive into your journey, but just like God had Peter's back, and Sandi's back, He'll have yours too, so no worries.

So what's your dream? Has God been trying to talk to you, but you haven't been ready to hear it yet? I believe you do know that you're pregnant, or you likely wouldn't be reading this book. You know that the fire is there but, what about the other messages that you may have been missing?

What usually happens when God is talking to us this way is that we simply wake up, get up, get dressed and go on with our day, as usual. It's just another ordinary day and nothing changes.

You may not think about your dream again. You might even forget all about the fact that you ever had it... at least until it happens again. And if you don't get it the first time, trust that it will come again. This I know from experience.

Now, Sandi's dream may not quite be your scenario, but I'll bet if you had a chance to share yours—the one that keeps coming back again and again—the ultimate message probably wouldn't be too far from Sandi's.

Here's the thing. There comes a time in most peoples' lives (and I'm guessing that time for you is now), where you recognize that there is something burning deep inside that you can't just turn off like a light switch. This thing is something that you have that's super special, even if you don't understand it all.

God may be trying to get a message to you. You won't always hear what He's saying with your natural ears. How is He talking to you? It's very important that you know so that you don't miss those important cues and clues that He's giving you throughout your day (and night). It's okay to ask Him to show you how He communicates with you. And when He tells you, make sure that you're listening.

Knock, and you will find. Seek, and the door of your understanding will be opened.

CHAPTER FOUR

WAIT! WHAT ABOUT TIMING? AM I READY FOR THIS?

"Just because you don't know anyone who has done it, doesn't mean that it's impossible to do."

Have you ever known anyone who delivered a baby and you never knew they were pregnant? Or perhaps it seemed as though they were only pregnant for a few months and the next thing you know, they're coming home with a newborn.

More than likely, most of the people in your circle know nothing of this fire you're carrying because you're very quiet about it. There may be a select few—those who are closest to you—who know bits and pieces, but even they only know what you're able to express with mere words. And usually, that's just a drop in the bucket—or more like a drop in the ocean.

The things you're feeling in your belly may not be that easy even for you to grasp right now, but do you realize that those deep yearnings aren't there by accident?

I know, sometimes we think that we came up with something really, really special that we want to do just because we're passionate about it. Passion is good, but what about purpose? What about destiny? Believe it or not, purpose and destiny play a huge part in where your passion lands. And your passion has a lot to do with where your destiny lands.

Have you ever thought about that "thing" that you're supposed to do until it got so huge that you talked yourself right out of it? Did it scare you? If it did, it's okay. You are definitely not alone. I've been there, too. I get it.

After all, who are YOU that something so great, so awesome, so amazing could actually be presented through you? Maybe you're not rich and famous, or perhaps you don't have the perfect body or the most beautiful smile in the world. Maybe you didn't attend any Ivy League schools or graduate in the top ten of your class. Or maybe you dropped out—or could it be that you didn't even go to college at all? And oh, God forbid if you didn't even manage to finish high school. No degree? No diploma? Certainly, nothing that great could come through you.

I hate to put your "no not me" button on pause, but here comes the real truth and it shouldn't surprise you.

If somebody somewhere in the world has achieved anything regardless of how difficult it may have been, that means it can be done. It also means that you could do it too, under the right circumstances. Again, it all boils down to the choices you make and how you apply yourself. There's also that slight chance that no one has done it yet because it's supposed to come through you.

Don't get me wrong here. I don't say this to mean you can do everything that everybody else does. But, here's a fact. You were born one day, and it wasn't an accident. The man and woman that God brought together to create you were brought together intentionally, regardless of who they are and how it turned out between them.

You can believe the way you wish, but I believe God had something to do with it. He doesn't make mistakes. In fact, I believe He created you to be a lot like Him, with no limitations.

If you're like most of us, life has taken its toll. Things haven't always gone in your favor and in some cases, life has been downright ugly and unfair.

People have said things about you that weren't true, and they may have laughed at you when you did something wrong or even when you did something right. You've had haters for no reason, and you've possibly even had a relationship... or two... or three... that went sour and left your heart slightly scarred.

Now you might be asking, "What kind of book did I just get? All of this doom and gloom. This book isn't at all what I was expecting." Don't worry; it lightens up soon. The truth is, we always have to start with what's real even when it's not all chocolate and marshmallows.

My guess is that if you're a lot like the rest of us, you may have experienced a few things in life that left you feeling less than a champion. If everything had gone your way, you most likely would already be walking in your truth and doing some amazing things.

So, what's my point in all of this? It certainly wasn't to bring you down and remind you of how bad things have gone for you. It was to let you know that your life probably lines up with 90% of the people in the world today. It also lines up with 99.9% of the people who have been through the same types of things and have stepped into their greatness—again, not necessarily because of it, but in spite of it.

See, sometimes we have this false belief that unless we come across as one shot less than perfect to everyone we meet, we can't accomplish great things. We have this false sense that only certain types of people can do big things. Believe me. When I say 'false' sense, I mean it with all of the passion you could imagine. The "perfect people" thing is a myth so don't think you have to wait until everything in your life is perfect before you can step into your greatness.

All It Takes to Rise Above Negative Circumstances Is to Make Good Choices.

If I had continued to allow my life to go in the direction that some people thought that it would, or even should, I'd still be "sitting on the dock of the bay watching the tide roll away." I don't have to think too long to know that I wasn't born just to sit and watch things happen. I wasn't born to observe everyone else accomplish their goals while I sat on the sidelines hoping that one day I could do something major, too.

As long as humanity exists, there will always be movers and shakers, lobbyists, rebels, and people who live to confront. There will be those who want to start movements, challenge mediocrity, ignorance, unfairness, starvation (I could go on). There are also those whose purpose could be very basic and simple and doesn't stir any major pots, but changes lives.

Here's what I mean. There will be those who should create or sell a product that helps people. There are those who have a gift or a service that could be a major benefit to others. There are those who should write a book, give a speech, start a podcast, create a blog or start a ministry. Their cause may not be so huge that the whole world finds out about it, but it still has a major effect on the lives of that specific group of people it will touch in some small way.

For some reason, most of us have the mindset that accomplishing great things is reserved for people with that "special" something, and not for those who fall into the category of "ordinary." Ordinary? What is an ordinary person?

An ordinary person has skin, bones, a heart, limbs and the use of their five senses. I'd say that's pretty accurate for ordinary (even if they have physical challenges). So what does a person have who does amazing things in the world? They have skin, bones, a heart, limbs and the use of their five senses. That's accurate too, but I think they have one more attribute that a lot of people lack.

They see themselves as great with an ability to do great things regardless of what anyone else might think, feel or believe about them. I like to put it this way. "People who make things happen, who dig deep and search for clear direction toward their destiny, are simply ordinary people who aren't afraid to do extraordinary things."

That means that maybe people who make things happen are not ordinary at all. There's something about their choices that sets them apart. And the fact that you're reading this book, I'm thinking you're not ordinary either.

Are You Beginning to Get a Little Clarity?

The reality is, I don't think you need convincing. You may just need clarification. I'm pretty certain that you have come to a point in your life where you do realize that you are good enough. You know beyond doubt that you do have something, and whatever is waiting for you in that body of water, you can handle it.

There came a time where I had such a deep yearning to help people do some of the things that I'd learned to do, that I became restless, agitated and downright irritated at doing nothing about it. I like to see people use their gifts and talents to help others do and be better. Sometimes the untapped potential that I'd see in people would almost frustrate me. Crazy... and wrong, but true. At times, I wasn't even sure why I was frustrated, but it was mostly because that "untapped potential" did not exclude me and where I lacked the drive to make something happen.

All I knew was that the things I'd been spending so much of my time on did not satisfy the "itch" or the "burning" in my own belly. Yes, I had a great career. I didn't hate my job, but I wasn't in love with it either. I knew I had responsibilities so not working at all was not an option for me.

I have a beautiful family. Married with kids, grandkids, and then some. As much joy and pleasure that I get from spending time with them, I knew there was still something more that I wanted, no... needed to do. In all honesty, I really couldn't put my finger on it. All I knew was... there's more. Much, more. God, what is it?

Now maybe for you, you've already passed that stage. Maybe you already fully understand what it is that you're called to do in life. If you're not 100% sure, no worries. It will come. I promise. The reality is you know that there's something. I can promise you this, too; until you start moving in the direction of what that "something" is, the restlessness, the longing for something more... will not disappear into thin air. It stays. Forever. Or at least until that "calling" is answered.

See, there's something about destiny and purpose. When you see both together as one thing, it's hard to separate the two. Destiny is going to happen anyway. If your purpose is linked to your destiny, you can't just toss it out as though it doesn't exist or just because it seems too hard to accomplish. However, you can choose not to walk in it because of what it will require of you. Just know that destiny and purpose don't leave your life just because you ignore them. Whether it's ignored for a season, a reason, or forever, your destiny will be, and your purpose is still meant to be, and it will wait for you. I hope this one didn't confuse you.

So, once you realize that you are supposed to be moving forward into something specific, what should your first step be? Since I believe in Jehovah God, I pray about everything I do at the very start, and I get answers. Praying is my personal choice, so please don't stop reading this book and miss out on what it has for you just in case we may not believe the same way.

Another thing I won't do in this book is, load you up with

a lot of fluff and empty words just to fill up the pages. My hope is that as you continue reading, you'll gain real direction and guidance on some tangible steps you can begin to take to get you closer to birthing the fire in your belly.

Why do I think I can help you? Remember... I've sat where you sit. I've been there, and I know what it is to wander around aimlessly, changing nothing and expecting something different to happen. Get clear that circumstances only change when you change.

First, you have to acknowledge that you indeed are pregnant with this "fire" that's in your belly. You have to know that there is something specific that your life is intended to affect. Whether it's been done or is currently being done by someone else doesn't matter. Birthing your fire is not about being in a competition. It's about you doing what you're called to do in the exact way that you are called to do it.

Let's look at it this way. Someone paints the picture of a beautiful flower. Everybody loves it. Another person may choose to paint the same flower. More people love it, and yet another paints the flower again. The point is, it's the same flower. Some people prefer the painting of the first artist. Others prefer artist number 2, and yet another group can't wait to get their eyes in front of the painting that the third artist created. Same flower, different artist, completely different experience, but the outcome is the same. Every person got the opportunity to enjoy the beauty of a painting that came from the heart and soul of the artist whose work they love.

My point is that you are uniquely you. I know you've heard that before, and I don't mean to sound stereotypical or redundant here, but it's truth. No one else in the entire universe can do what God has called YOU to do in the way that He has called YOU to do it.

Also, no one else can reach or connect with people—a certain group of people—in the same way that YOU can. It doesn't matter whether your calling is to cut hair, design garments, build houses, lead a ministry, or start a movement that could change the world. What you're supposed to be doing can only be done the way you're supposed to do it.

Know that everything you have learned and experienced from the day you were born up to this point in your life has great meaning. I mentioned earlier about some things that may have happened to you that were a bit unpleasant. None of us like to dwell on those negative things.

But remember that you might be called to take all of the messes that you've endured, all of the things that you were once a victim of and turn them into your message, especially if you have overcome them. Do you realize that there are tens of thousands of others in the world who would love to know how you did it? There's something about people who win and beat the odds that's intriguing. We all love seeing the "Cinderella" effect that takes place in a life that overcomes, even though our experiences may be far from their story.

The scripture found in Ecclesiastes 1:9 says "there is nothing new under the sun" so if you've been through it, dealt with it, overcome it, I would assume that many others are right now struggling with it. They don't have the answers. They don't know the solution, but you do. They don't know how to cope, what to do, how to "be" but you've figured it out. Don't think so? Aren't you still standing? Even if you're a little wobbly, you're standing and that counts for a lot.

You don't have to be a super-hero.

Sometimes we think that a purpose, calling, or assignment is something that's so far-fetched that we need to become almost "super-human" to carry it out. Do you realize that even the smallest accomplishment is HUGE in the eyes of the person who's still trying to figure it all out? So never take the lessons you've learned, the path you've walked, the challenges you've overcome as a little thing that no one would care about.

Your life has meaning and purpose. HUGE purpose—and if there's a message in there, (and there usually is), thousands of people are waiting to hear it.

There is a specific group of people who need your help. They need your understanding about a certain matter. They need to know that as bad as it may have gotten for them, there really is a way out. How will they know? You're going to tell them your story. You're going to let them know that you made it and that they can too.

You know, sometimes we don't have to look very far to realize that the fire that's been burning in our bellies for so many years started way before we knew anything about purpose. It started in the hard times, in the rough times and in the not so happy times.

It started when as a little child, crying on the front porch because you dealt with another day of bullying or you're tired of hearing your parents fight. You think those things only happen in the movies? That may or may not be your story or mine, but it happens in real life every day.

Maybe this "purpose" started when you dealt with that

illness, whether it was yours or someone close to you. It was real, and it was a difficult time, and you're still here. Or perhaps it started with the death of someone near and dear. We didn't know how we could ever live without them, but we're still here. It's hard, but we're here.

Never discount the hand that you've been dealt. You're a winner and whether or not you know it, you're worth your weight in gold and then some—as the kids used to say... "All that and a bag of chips." Your life means something. Something great.

Even though you may not be 100% clear on what the little fire that's stewing in your belly is all about, God is clear. And it's my belief that as you continue reading this book, it will become more clear to you. Not only will your purpose become clearer, but once it's revealed, you won't be left in the dark about what to do next.

It's your time, and I couldn't be more excited for you. You've been pregnant a long time. Your labor is about to begin and you will soon deliver this baby. Or should I say, this fire in your belly is about to be released into the world!

You know that you, yes even you... an (extra)ordinary person, can have and be all about purpose. You can be all about extraordinary things. It's YOUR purpose, your gift, your knowledge... no one else's.

Now that you know, let's help you stop doing things to squash those delivery pains and finally go through the delivery process to get that fire birthed into the world that it is sent to change.

Where do you start? Start with ignoring all the things

you've been told and believed about yourself that don't line up with where you're wanting to go.

CHAPTER FIVE

◆◆◆◆◆◆◆◆◆◆◆

DROWNING OUT THE NOISES IN MY HEAD!

"Don't let those head noises speak louder than the voice that's speaking truth."

I remember growing up as a child... one of the things I wanted for sure was to do well in school. I got good grades. I would quickly grasp most of what my teachers said, and I got it without trying very hard. Too bad I didn't understand the importance of applying myself more. I could have been a straight "A" student.

By the time I got to high school, I knew that I wanted to be a school teacher. I knew that I would be good at it and that I would love being the one to help somebody else learn something new because I enjoyed learning so much. Learning felt good to me even then. I say then because to this day, I continue to invest in learning and being trained and mentored by top notch coaches who help me better understand what I need to know so I can be just as helpful, if not more, as I coach others.

But before all of that, somewhere in those high school years, a lot of noise started to happen. The positive belief that I'd had as a young girl was slowly starting to fade. It didn't cause me to give up on my dream, but that bright light that I had once been so excited about, that light that kept me going, started to grow a little dim. After all, everything that the kids say is always true, right? Well, for me it felt that way, and I was constantly reminded of it.

See, even though I didn't grow up in a family that had a lot of money, my folks instilled in me that I could be whatever I wanted to be in life. They let me know that if I would apply myself, I could do anything, and I believed them.

But the "noise" that I got from the high school kids was a completely different conversation. It said…

"You're so skinny."

"You're the ugliest person I've ever seen."

"Hey, black pepper." (My last name was Peppers)

I could talk about the 'not so nice' things the kids said for days, but why waste my time on that. Let's just say, going to high school started not to be fun at all. I suppose that I could have survived some of the negative things that were constantly flung at me, but at age 15, what are you going to do besides take it to heart and start believing it.

The words were bad enough; but when the actions followed, that's when it started to sting. I wasn't popular… The boys didn't want to date me… The girls didn't like me…

After all, I was a 'church girl.' I didn't smoke in the bathroom with the other kids, I didn't pop 'red-devils,' (the popular drug of the day), I didn't curse people out at the drop of a hat and I wasn't loud and obnoxious. Get the picture? Yes, I'm the skinny little church girl who ended up so shy and withdrawn that I had no idea how to act when I finally got permission to go on my first date. He took me out to dinner, and I was too shy to eat in front of him. Wow... really? Yes... that was me. The meal was wasted and so was his money.

I was a junior in high school before I went to my first dance and that was a Coronation Ball. I made my dress (and boy did it look home-made), and I had to be home by 11 or 11:30. My date was the geek guy that all the other girls had said no to. He couldn't get a date either, but guess who was still available! Yep, that would be me. And even though he was the school geek (for guys) he ignored me the whole time we were there. I can't say that I blame him. Honestly, my dress was hideous. Thankfully, I can laugh about it now.

But I can say... the teachers liked me, but that made it even worse. "Awe... she's just the teacher's pet, that's why she gets good grades..." No. I think it's called studying and turning in your homework on time but I didn't have the guts to say it.

At this point in school, I'm not caring so much. I started doing my own thing by myself or with the couple of friends that I did have, at least until I became a senior. This year was supposed to be fun, right? But wait—the same kids who didn't like me when I was a freshman still don't like me now, so what's the difference. Nothing, except I'm a few years older now. I was still too chicken to party like everybody else and oddly enough, I really didn't want to. And I don't think it was because I was so into God at the time. As a matter of fact, I know that wasn't it. I was more afraid of what I thought my folks would do to me if I ever got caught. I'd go into detail, but let's just say that things back in the day were so much different than they are today.

When I really think about it, I'd say that almost all of our parents from those days would be underneath jail cells if the same things were done to kids today that was done to us back then. But I have to admit, if I had to do it all again, I wouldn't change a thing. Today, I truly understand discipline, and it has served me well.

And although I've had amazing accomplishments in my adult life, during those earlier years, the noise had gotten much louder than all of the years of positivity that had been poured into me. So much so that I started to believe the negative noises over anything else I'd been told.

The year I became a junior in high school, I would meet a young man that would completely change my life. I met him when I was 16, and he was 22. My father warned me that he was too old for me and was probably a lot more "experienced" than me.

Back then, they didn't just come out and tell you what that meant, but I would soon learn. "Experience' meant that he'd done things with "fast" girls that I knew absolutely nothing about.

All I knew was, he didn't call me names. As a matter of fact, he told me how beautiful he thought I was, and he'd never met anyone like me. These words were the complete opposite of the noise I'd been hearing from the kids at school. I was all ears.

Whenever he would pick me up from school in his bright shiny red and white Riviera, I felt like a queen. Nobody else had a boyfriend like this, just me. I finally felt noticed. I finally felt "good enough." So yes, look at me now! I've got the cool guy and you girls have dorks who still have pimples. Look at me now!!

Right. Look at me now. I'm now 18 and graduating from high school in January. Not just because I made good grades and had enough credits, but I needed to be home so I could have my beautiful baby.

But this is where the noise gets real loud. I'm not just the church girl who's now knocked up. I'm also the church musician, the president of the youth group, the "upstanding" perfect little preacher's kid who doesn't drink, smoke or do drugs; well preacher's niece, but it was still all the same.

My aunt and uncle were the 'social elite' in our Christian community. Everybody knew and loved them. They were famous in the district, and they were perfect. And I was perfect. (Hope you got the sarcasm here)... at least on my part.

Lordy, Lord, Who on earth am I and what in the world have I done? I'm this perfect little "church girl" who does no wrong, with a perfect aunt and uncle who do no wrong (they honestly didn't as far as I knew). And to this day, I love them both to pieces for the example they set. But all that said, what am I, the perfect little church girl supposed to do now?

What about my dream to become a school teacher and the "assignment" given to me to lead the other young ladies in this amazing Christian walk? What about college? What about my scholarship? What about my aunt and uncle and what about mom? Mom, you're coming to visit at the worst possible time. And oh God... what about my dad who I just know is going to kill me the minute he finds out? All of this is way too crazy. What about all of these church people who I know are going to judge me hard?

So now my mind is running a hundred miles a minute. In addition to the school kids not liking me, the church kids now don't like me because their parents told them not to. After all, I'm now the "bad" girl. The "grown- ups" have now turned on me because I was supposed to be the "goody-two-shoes" example for their bad kids and I somehow 'failed them.'

"Hey... what about your kids who party every weekend and come to church hungover on Sundays?" What about that girl that got pregnant and nobody said anything just because her family wasn't in the limelight? Huh? What about her? Oh yes, I almost forgot... I was the "PK" and I'm supposed to be perfect. Right.

In my mind, I even believed that my family wouldn't love me anymore. After all, they told me about my "friend," and I didn't listen, so how could they still love me? Note: I was WAY wrong. They loved me through it all even though my head said they would hate me.

Noise. Noise. Noise. Oh, and get this... The doctor who "verified" my pregnancy even suggested that I be 'sent away' until I deliver my baby—(that's what they did back in the day if you had a baby and weren't married.) Of course, the guys never got sent away... just the bad girls. Go figure. Oh yes, and that good-looking young man that made me feel so special and important? Well, he decided that it was time to move to another state to go on a "hunt" for his "real father" the minute he found out I was having a baby. Wow, really?

This is really happening?

And when he did come back to town the week that I had my daughter, my preacher uncle was so mad at him for leaving me to deal with everything by myself that he pulled a gun on him and ran him off for good. (Not that he was there to stay... but, who knows.) Yes, this was my perfect little life.

My sweet uncle (who turned 100 in 2017) and I kind of chuckle about it now. And when I introduced my amazing husband to the handsome young man and his wife many years later, we all chuckled about it too, but it sure wasn't funny back then.

Reflecting back on that time, standing there with all of the responsibility of being a single teen mom hanging over my head, I felt that all of my dreams of being anybody, doing anything special, teaching school, being a leader, going to or finishing college went right down the drain into the abyss.

Now, it's about survival. All of the noise around me still assured me that I was no longer good enough to expect to do anything more than struggle to provide for my sweet baby girl and me.

I started to doubt whatever ability I had developed. And, I certainly didn't think anyone else would ever want to listen to anything I'd have to say, even if I was their teacher.

Yes, circumstances can change, people change, situations change and surroundings can change. All of those changes can have a strong, strong effect on what you hear in your head and heart. In case you're not aware, your heart and your mind are one in the same when it comes to your feelings, emotions, and beliefs.

There is a scripture that says "as a man thinks, so is

he...?" That means that what you believe about yourself is how you will respond to everything in life. It dictates all of your actions; it determines the line of work that you choose; it causes you to either move forward with your purpose or believe the noisy lies that were created to drown out your truth. And, if you're not careful, it will even cause you to change the type of people that you start to hang around.

It's been said that people tend to hang around people who are most like them. Not those who are most like who and what they would like to be. So how do you picture yourself? What's the conversation of the people that you hang around the most? Does their conversation line up with where you want to go? If not, there's a problem brewing that may need to be corrected.

I remember that as long as I had to go to school and listen to the noise that the kids would say, then go to church and listen to the noise that the church people would say, I couldn't figure out what my own voice was trying to say. It got completely drowned out. So what ended up happening?

The voices and noise (and noise is exactly what it is), of everybody else became my new reality. Notice I didn't say truth. Reality and truth are not always synonymous. My truth was never that I no longer wanted to be a teacher or that I was no longer capable. My new (false) reality told me that I no longer could be, so don't bother trying.

I thought I had overcome the noise.

After some time had passed, I mustered up enough courage to give college a try. I was going to go ahead and get my degree and credentials to become a school teacher after all. That's what I'd always wanted to do. I started a program that was part of a scholarship I'd received. I was knee-deep in one of the programs that would help me with my college credits. Perfect! I can finally do what I've wanted to do since I was a child—before I messed up... or thought I had.

While in the program, I was assigned to an elementary classroom as a teachers' aide, and I loved it. I was there for just a couple of months. One day, the teacher had an emergency and was not going to be coming in. Instead of the principal replacing her with a "real" experienced teacher, because I'd been doing such a good job, he decided to give me the class for the entire day. I was in a class of 8th graders, who ALL happened to be bigger than me. (I was a still a puny little thing back then.)

One of the students decided that none of them should have this skinny little person telling them what to do. I'm thinking, why won't they listen to me? The teacher had a lesson plan that I knew how to follow so why shouldn't they allow me (this person who physically looked younger than all of them), tell them what or how to do these assignments? Isn't that the way it's supposed to go?

Well, the students didn't see it that way, so they decided that rather than listen to me, they would beat me up after school. I still, can't figure out what that was supposed to prove, but back then, that was something that was very popular with the more rowdy kids. They didn't shoot people up back then. They just beat people up after school while everybody stood around and watched and cheered for their favorite opponent.

At any rate, here I am once again. The students in the classroom don't like me. I haven't done anything to them, and they still don't like me. It brought up everything that I'd ever felt from high school, from church, from friends... only magnified even more because I didn't do anything to warrant this. The noise in my head got so loud; I made a rash decision that day. Not the right one (I would find that out later)... but one that would seal my fate and change the course of my entire life forever.

You think you're going to beat me up after school? Think again. It's not going to happen. Why? That's easy because I won't be here. When the bell rang for lunch break, I grabbed all of my belongings and walked out without saying a word to anyone. I didn't get clearance from the principal, I didn't speak to any of the other teachers, and I left the students without a teacher.

From that day, I would never return to traditional college or my desire to be a school teacher. In my mind, all I heard was, "if this is what I have to deal with to become a teacher, you can have it. I'm done."

And, I don't think I left because I was so afraid of the beat down. What I remembered most was that "feeling" stirring up again... those memories—the noise of rejection. At that time, I'd experienced so much rejection I just couldn't handle it. I think somewhere in my thoughts I heard... you can hit me, just don't reject me.

I know... you may be saying, "That's really not too bad." You're absolutely right. This is pretty menial in comparison to what many have experienced. If I tried to tell you all of my story here, you'd never pick up this book because it would be too thick.

Now, fast forward to what sometimes feels like a million years later.

Teaching was not just my passion or my dream. It was

then and still is part of my purpose, calling, mission and ministry. So even though all of the noises that rang so loud in my head told one story, the truth of my destiny and calling never changed.

It didn't matter that I chose to walk away. So what. I may have walked away from something physically, but what God put me on this earth to do, that "thing" that I was formed in the womb to do, never changed. Everything that I would do from that point on would still find me teaching. Whether on a job, in business, or ministry, I somehow would fall right back to that place. Sharing, teaching, helping someone learn something that would enhance their life in some small way.

I learned a profound lesson in all of this. You may walk away from your purpose even if you feel you have a valid reason. But your purpose never walks away from you or the plan that God intended for your life. It may go on pause for a moment, or possibly even delayed, but it never goes away.

That vision you have belongs to you.

There will be times in your life where it feels like you are the only one who believes in you. The people around you don't see what you see. The vision that you have will be completely foreign to them. Sometimes, your vision is so big that others will think that your mind is a little out of whack to think that you could accomplish such a thing.

After all, what makes you think that YOU could do something so great? When did YOU, the skinny, ugly, wallflower, pregnant out of wedlock quitter, become somebody that would ever have anything to offer to anyone?

In the minds of those who don't believe in you, you're just like them. You're too familiar. You get up, go to school or work, come home and make dinner or eat out, watch a little television, then go to bed, and get up and do the very same thing the same way the next day, and the next day, and the next day...

Don't buy into the lies or noises from outside forces!

Those noises aren't coming from you or anything that God has put inside you. And if you listen too long, you'll end up unhappy, unfulfilled, depressed and angry. Just stop listening. I'm convinced that you don't have a mediocre mindset, or you wouldn't still be reading this book right now.

There will be those times that nobody, and I do mean NOBODY else, believes in you. Should that change your path? Not if it's the path that you know without a doubt that you're supposed to travel.

This path is where you have to learn how to tell the naysayers to get out of your way. Tell the haters to go and hate somewhere else because their feelings toward you have no bearing on who you are called to be or how you're supposed to show up in the world.

Your job is to keep your heart and mind focused on the path that you know you should be traveling. Learn what you need to learn and do the work that you need to do so that you can move forward.

Do you realize that when you're on a path, and you stop moving in that direction, you're the one who makes the choice to turn and go a different way? Others may do and say things that might discourage you from taking forward steps, but YOU are the only one who can make the decision to keep yourself heading in the right direction. You choose which fork in the road you will take—no one else.

Even if you've given up at some point, your destiny and purpose are still waiting for you. God created you to be the person He has called, designed, and destined you to be.

Life does cause us sometimes to travel down some roads that we'd rather avoid, but here's another truth. God does not make mistakes. What He intended for you ten years ago... 20 years ago... 50 years ago still stands today.

He doesn't lie and is not one to change. What He said about you before the foundations of the earth were laid still rings true today. What was proclaimed for you from day one is already a done deal. You can't change that truth, but you can change the outcome. All you have to do is drown out all of the noise that is designed to keep you stuck. So, you might be wondering how you're supposed to forget the past and start with a clean slate. You don't.

Your past is a very vital part to your present and your future. The things you've experienced in life are no accident. You've been dealt some cards that from face value, don't seem at all like a winning hand. But you were never created to lose, no matter how it sometimes looks or feels.

I took a whole chapter to share some small portions of my past not just because I haven't forgotten them. I use them to remind me that my life, my story, can be the bridge that someone else can use to cross over to their other side just like someone did for me.

I'll say it again. Don't forget your past. Use your past to serve others and catapult you into your future. If your life has been a mess, turn it into a message that could change somebody's life.

CHAPTER SIX

♦♦♦♦♦♦♦♦♦♦♦

SHOULD I REALLY TELL MY STORY?

"Who would have ever thought that all of those mess-ups could become your best message?"

So, who wants to be vulnerable anyway? I certainly didn't. Not for a minute. And I don't exaggerate when I tell you that it would be decades before I would get to a place where I would be okay letting people into my past reality. It wasn't because I'm not a good person or because I was ashamed... or was I?

Before I stepped into my own purpose, I really hadn't given much thought at all—if any—to the things I'd gone through. I'd lived through them, and I was used to them. I'd come out of them, and it was all a thing of the past. All of it. This was *my* life, *my* experiences and *my* business and anyway, who cared? I had never looked at the challenges that I'd faced as anything that could benefit somebody else. In my mind, none of it was an advantage to me, so why would I even consider that it could help anyone else?

What I didn't realize was that sharing my story would be a major part of my ministry. Really? I don't have a "woe is me"—"poor little me" ministry. After all, I teach people about business, wealth, and prosperity for goodness sakes. Who wants to hear about negative stuff? And who knew that the challenges I'd come through would also play a part in the success of my own business?

At first, I didn't understand how my life could be an example for anybody. I shared much of my story in the last chapter, but at the core of it all, it's a story of how a young girl started out with many challenges, was faced to make new choices, and ended up with the life of her dreams.

Yes, there was a period of my childhood that I ate beans for dinner almost every day. I bought everything I owned from the local Goodwill center (and not because I liked "vintage" styling but because I didn't have much choice). I still remember when I was elementary school age and wanted to go swimming at our neighborhood pool with the other kids. I didn't have a bathing suit, but I remember my brother taking me to the Goodwill and we found a shiny red bathing suite for 25 cents. I still remember exactly what it looked like and how thrilled I was because I had the quarter I needed to buy it—not to mention that I also got to go swimming.

That was no big deal to me at the time. However, I've found that something as noneventful as having no money for a child sized bathing suit to being able to dine out whenever I want, travel and have no debt, could show another person that there is hope. It shows the person who has that story today that it doesn't matter at all how you start. Things can truly turn around when you take the right steps.

Because I overcame my rejection issues, I actually forgot that I even had that story. So, to my point, everybody has a story and my guess is that yours will help more people than you know… but only if you share it.

When I did share certain parts of my story for the first time, I was a guest speaker for a women's ministry. I hadn't planned on sharing my "stuff" at all. All I did was prayed and ask God for direction on what He wanted me to share. When I began to prepare, my story came out. Wow, God… really???

If you have a hard time trying to discover what your story is, it's probably that one thing that you've swept so far under the rug that you've almost forgotten that it existed. What's that part of your life that you would dread for people to know about? Or, what about that part of your life that's so far in the distance now, that it never crosses your mind anymore?

In many ways, it's great that you don't think about it. If you haven't just drowned it out or covered it up, it means that you've truly overcome and have learned how to walk in real victory. You're no longer dwelling in your past, but you've learned to live in the here and now; looking toward the future. That's good. But what if you had to dig it up so it could help someone else? Could you live with the memories and still be okay?

I know that this goes against the grain of what most people would say to you, and I get it. It almost doesn't make sense. Why dig up the past, especially if it's not something to be celebrated. But—did you come through it? Then, it should be celebrated. Don't look at it as digging up the past so you can wallow in it again. If it can help you get closer to that purpose that we've been talking about; that fire that needs to be birthed, you may have to go digging.

I know it seems like the craziest thing to put yourself out there in a way that would expose your truth. I always tell people that I work with that you should know your boundaries and stick with them. However, my belief is that often, your truth is the very thing that can put you smack dab in the middle of your purpose.

So, how do you share your story without being afraid? First, you have to come to the point where you accept your story, good or bad. Yes, that was your life at one time but remember; you came through it.

On the other hand, there are many who seem to have had an almost perfect life, and therefore feel that they don't have a story. This could be you. Don't be embarrassed if most people around you didn't have your same experience. If you weren't poor, never had to wonder where your next meal would come from, always had enough money to pay your bills or didn't suffer at all, be thankful.

Reality is that many people in the world have never experienced lack in any area and still are looking for peace or something they don't currently have. Problems don't always come in the form of financial woes and physical or mental abuse. In your case, just find out who the people are that can best resonate with where you've been. Most often, the story you have to share will largely determine who the people are that you are called to serve.

When you think of who these people are, find out what

questions they have and answer them. What problems do they have for which you have found the solution? And remember, it doesn't have to be negative. As long as you have discovered a solution to a problem or found an answer to a question, you have something to share.

As you're preparing to birth your fire, ask yourself this question. "What initially started this fire to rumble in my belly?" Knowing this will usually help you to determine what part of your story you should tell. What if you have multiple stories? Not a problem. You may have so much life experience or knowledge that you think you have too much to share. Always know that whatever you choose to share at any given time, needs to be incredibly relatable to the people you will speak to. And that goes for business and ministry.

Know that as you do share, you have to become so vulnerable it almost makes you uncomfortable, at least at first. I say at first because the more you share, the more comfortable you will become. Trust me on that one.

Let me get back to what I mentioned earlier. When I first shared my simple little story at that women's meeting, after it was all over I sat down, and it hit me. "What did I just do?" I laid it all out there. Now they know the "real" me... not the me that I'd been showing them for all those years.

They knew that I'd married more than once and that one ex-husband was once gay and probably should have never taken a wife. These ladies also found out that I was away from my mom (who they all knew) for some of my childhood years. I could go on and on about all that I shared that day, but I won't. We'll save ALL of that for another time. And yes, there's more. Lot's more.

After I'd spoken that day, I questioned everything I had shared. Why did I do it? Why did I lay it all out there for people to start now judging and rejecting me... again? My thought was if I could only take it all back. God, "WHY DID YOU MAKE ME DO THIS?"

Well, it was done and right afterwards, I felt like finding a hole to crawl into. My stuff was out there now, and there wasn't anything I could do to take it back. I braced myself for all the backlash that would come as a result. But it never happened. As a matter of fact, I remember how light and free I felt when I finished and how surprisingly (once I took a deep breath and took it all in) I didn't regret sharing my "stuff" at all. I actually felt a freedom that I'd never experienced before and now, it felt good.

When that conference was over, I had more women waiting to speak with me than I'd ever had before. And might I add, some of them were people I'd known for years. Who would have thought... Some had tears in their eyes as they were thanking me for being so real and vulnerable. Huh? They're not looking down on me? I didn't get it at first.

I always wanted to come across as this pulled together "Super Woman" with no issues, no problems... everything is looking and "feeling" just right. That's how I'd been my whole life. I discovered something very, very important that day. The more people can identify with you, the more they can relate and will trust you! And the more they trust you, the more they will feel comfortable enough to move forward with you in more areas like business or ministry.

I had always thought that the "better" I came across, being all of that and then some, the more they would accept me. If I "appeared" to have it all together, people would really like me and I wouldn't have to experience that rejection again. Boy, did I have that wrong.

What I came to realize that day is that the more that people could see my authenticity and the more that they could see some things that we had in common, the more freedom they felt when they were around me. They could be themselves without feeling that they would be judged by me. In their mind, I was just like them but "appeared" to now be so pulled together.

My point is simple. Don't be afraid to tell your story and whatever you do, be authentic. Don't try to pretend that you have arrived if you haven't. And if you have, you don't need to downplay yourself, but know who you're reaching out to and learn how to meet them right where they are.

Keep in mind that your audience will need to get a clear picture of who you are, where you've been, what you've come through and where you're headed next. I know… that's a lot. And the truth is, sometimes we don't even know all of these things ourselves. But that should never stop us from being willing to move forward in our honest to goodness truth. In a nutshell, just be authentic. It will take you far.

While you want the people you want to connect with to see that you have *now* arrived, that's just to show them that they can too. You also want them to see that at one point in your life, you weren't on top of the mountain. You may not have always been successful, and maybe, just maybe… you were once exactly where they are right now.

Of course, keep all of this in perspective with your message. Always know who you're talking to and how the things that you do or say can have a major impact on the lives of those you will touch. When you think about that fire that's in your belly, you've got to know who it's burning for. Yes, the fire is *in* you, but it's *for* somebody else. It's for someone else's victory, someone else's breakthrough, somebody else's success!

Will it be hard to put yourself out there at first? Absolutely. But if you really want to reach the right people, those that your fire is burning for, it's a necessity. I'm not sure why it is, but there is something about humanity that says... "You're sort of like me. Now I am more willing not just to hear you, but I'm ready to pay close attention to what you have to say."

Please don't get me wrong. I can't stress this one enough. You *can* set limits, and you *do* need boundaries. Only you and God know how far you should go into your story. I say, when you're truly free there are no worries, even if you go deep. I hope you can understand my point here. It's very simple.

1. Don't be afraid to tell your story.

2. Don't be fake and phony about anything. People can see through it and they won't like it.

3. Don't worry about the backlash you'll get (and yes, you will get some.)

4. Learn to move in strength and vulnerability at the same time.

If you can latch on to these fundamental principles, you'll be amazed at how you will start to shape and form who you are becoming in your purpose. Understand too, when it comes to destiny and purpose, these things usually have nothing to do with being shallow or all about you. When you put yourself out there, it's just par for the course.

So what if you're ready, but you don't know where to start? This is where we go to work.

First... take some time to reflect.

Take a back-peek at your past and bring to the forefront of your mind, the ten most important events that have happened in your life. I remind you—don't make the mistake of thinking that everything about your story has to be negative or bad.

When you're sharing your story, you always want to let people know that it ends well, even if you went through hell. And... if it didn't end well, you MUST be able to pull up some of the good and positive things that have happened in your life. Yes, as bad as some of the bad might have been, never leave out the good. People love happy endings to a story, so don't leave them sad and feeling sorry for you.

When you think about your purpose, look for the positive outcome, and an uplifting message. Find something that shows people that there is light at the end of that dark tunnel, whether it's the one you've come through or the one they're currently going through. Remember, the life you've lived is not just for you. You certainly don't want to waste all the drama you've had to deal with. Use it for the good of someone else.

When you start to think about these ten things, look at each one as a complete and separate story. In many cases, I know that one story will overlap into another, and that's okay, but separate as much as you can. You might ask why isn't your life just one big story. Well, because if you're like most people, you've dealt with more than one situation. Remember, one part of your story will relate to one group of people and another part will relate to another group.

As you share, whether you are writing a book, sharing a message or having a conversation with someone about them purchasing a product or service from you, you want to make sure you're sharing the things that you believe are most relevant to that person. You want to share something that will have the most impact on the lives of a particular group of people but always have one individual in your mind, even if you don't know her personally. It will still resonate with the group if you're thinking of the right person.

What does your story have to do with birthing the fire in your belly?

I don't know what you're called to do. I don't know who you're called to teach, serve, coach or influence in some way. What I do know is that every intent you have, whether it's business, pleasure, ministry or something else, goes back to the root of why I wrote this book. You do have purpose, and it's not just for your benefit. It's about helping other people and anytime other people are involved, a level of connection is involved even more. Your audience absolutely MUST be able to relate. Without this, you will find that your purpose is not being released where it needs to be.

It's time to come out of hiding. It's necessary and it won't be as difficult as you may think. Don't allow your desire to be so "private" and perfect in everyone's eyes keep you from being effective in your message. Being vulnerable in the right place, at the right time, does not make you weak. It's the cowardly who hide, not the strong at heart.

Again, don't ignore your boundaries. Pick the stories that you are willing to share and allow them to change lives all over the world.

CHAPTER SEVEN

✦✦✦✦✦✦✦✦✦✦

THEY MAY CALL YOU STRANGE, BUT ALWAYS REMAIN UNIQUELY YOU!

"Whatever you're called to do in life, no one can deliver your gift to the world the way you can."

It's pretty impressive when extraordinary things happen in the world. What's a little perplexing is that when these things do happen, people are usually shocked to think that such awesomeness could actually come through people within their own personal circles or those that they are extremely familiar with.

After all, getting back to that "ordinary people" thing, most people have the mindset that says "where I live" no one does anything special. That's usually because they believe that where they live, everyone is supposed to be just like them. We get so accustomed to doing everything status quo with the same group of people that we don't ever expect anyone to rise up and do something fantastic.

Although we may recognize that someone within our group has a little something special, we don't challenge or encourage them to step out from the crowd, away from the ordinary and do that extraordinary thing. More often than not, most people would respond to a big thinker with that all too familiar look that says... "You're kidding, right?" I wonder why that is.

Is it because we have placed such limitations on ourselves that we somehow figure that those we hang around the most are just like us? We do what we're told, how we're told, when we're told and very little above or beyond what is expected. Here's a clue. Nobody who has done anything amazing, great, or extraordinary has done what was expected by the masses around them.

We already know that we will get together and go to the movies every other Friday and have pizza afterward, or we'll go to the "all you can eat" buffet after church on Sunday. We shop at the same stores and even buy the same style of clothing over and over again. How do I know? Has anyone ever said to you something like... "I saw this dress at the XYZ boutique, and it looked just like you. You've got to see it. I know you'll like it."

Why did they say that? Because of what I just stated earlier. We are creatures of habit. We buy the same thing, do the same thing, we think the same way because it's what we know and where we are comfortable.

Once we get conformed to a particular mold, we feel at home in it and very rarely do we try to change it. As a rule, we don't like change. We like the "knowing" of what's familiar. Have you ever heard the challenge to take a different route home from work, just to break the routine? Did you do it? Congrats if you did. Most people don't.

Big works in the world are for "those people."

Do "those people" have some supernatural power or a secret that the rest of us know nothing about? Is it because they chose to step outside of the box that causes us to look at them a little strange—or if it's you, they look at you a little strange? Or, is it that we have such limiting beliefs that it just doesn't seem realistic that someone that we sit at the dinner table with, ride to work with, or workout at the gym with, could be the next person to start a movement that could change the world.

I'll never forget the day that I saw a news anchor that was in my third grade class in elementary school. It was the oddest thing. I jumped off the sofa and said... "Hey!! I went to school with that girl!

I still remember how it felt when someone I'd known personally actually ended up becoming a TV personality. To me, my former classmate was now famous. Well... let's say famous in my hometown of St. Louis, Missouri. How did she do that? How does someone from my neighborhood that I went to school with, end up becoming a news anchor seen on television every day?

Always keep in mind that regardless of what a person does, everybody is somebody's childhood friend, sibling, parent or neighbor. The reality is that I was where I was because of the choices I'd made for my life. Good, bad or indifferent, they were my choices. And she was where she was because of the choices that she made for hers.

So, why should I be surprised because someone that I know personally is doing something extraordinary? Why not YOU or ME be the one who steps outside of the ring and does something that's uniquely us... something great that nobody would ever expect!

Bring your unique gift to the table.

I've already said this, but I feel that I should say it again. There is not another person on this whole planet, not even in the universe who is exactly like you. Your fingerprints are identical to no one else's. Just like you are unique, so is your gift to the world.

Whatever it is that you are called, appointed, anointed, or hand-selected to do, know that there are thousands of others who have a similar purpose, but no one will ever deliver whatever your gift is exactly the way you will.

What you have been given to present to the world may not be unique at its core, but because you are like no one else, when you present it, it will be presented in a way that only you can. And when you do present it, never try to copy or be an exact mirror of someone else. Yes, it's great to learn from others and gain an understanding of the concepts that work.

It's a good thing to glean from what speaks to your soul, or someone who is successful in what you want to do, but don't steal. Learn. Soak it all up then release it in your own way. Once you understand something and put it into practice for yourself, it becomes yours. Now, take it and do you.

When you read the things I say in this chapter, I don't want you to get the impression that no one can do what you do better than you. You will always find people who do things better. And, it doesn't mean that everybody else who has something similar should step aside so that only YOU can shine. Absolutely not! What I mean is that you may have something to share that a million others have shared, but for many, the way it comes from you is the only way they'll receive it. Let me try to put an English spin on this so that you get a clear understanding. And here, I'm going to allude to something that I've mentioned earlier.

Everybody has preferences. You can get ten grandmas in a room, each with their own apple pie recipe. No doubt, they will all be very good. But for you, there will be one that tastes so good you'll feel like you're wasting your time sampling the rest. You want the one that you want, or you want none at all. Plain and simple.

Take all of the television shows. Let's hone in on reality shows that are so popular these days. When you get right down to it, there aren't a lot of differences between them. They all include a cast of people who have some issue that takes them through drama after drama, fight after fight, episode after episode, before it's ever solved, if ever.

The premise is very similar and so is the message, or let's say lack of. But, some people like this show and others like that one. Another group prefers yet a different one. What separates one from the other isn't the story line, but the character and personalities of the people who are telling the story with their lives... scripted or real. It goes right back to the artists who painted the flowers or an individual who sings the same song that five others sang.

I don't want to pound this one too hard because it was talked about earlier, but I do want you to get a real understanding of how important it is to allow yourself to be uniquely you. Your uniqueness may seem strange to some people, but that very "strange" uniqueness about you is the very thing that will catapult you to exactly where you need to be.

I saw the same similarity as I was writing this book. I'm sure that the things you've read here, you have heard a dozen times before. My voice is for those who can relate to my voice. Some will "catch" the message this time who never got it before.

I wrote this book because when I speak on stages, I found that people would often want more. It's not because they haven't heard my message before, but they related to my uniqueness. The message was not unique because what I said was better or different than what someone else said. It was unique because it was me, an individual, who used my voice and personality to share the message.

My desire is that after I have spoken, I can leave people with this book (and the accompanying workbook) that will give them something more to latch on to. My hope is that this book will keep them thinking and dreaming long after I have left their stages. I want them (and you) to come to the realization that you have significant worth in the world and that sitting on your gift is the last thing you should ever be doing. Ever!

Again, my point is simple. You will stand out from the crowd to the people that you appeal to the most. And you'll be different than many of the people in your immediate circles unless your circles are full of people who are willing to start walking in their truth just like you are.

Because of this, when you sit in front of your computer for hours at a time to write that book instead of going out with the group, your family and friends won't get it. When you spend most of your free time educating yourself on how to do something well, or at least better than you know how to do it right now, they may just look at you and shake their heads, or send you that 'smh' text.

It's strange to them because it's different than what they expect from you. The sad part is, many of those who don't get why you do what you do are not satisfied with their current situations either. They've just made the choice to continue doing things status quo. Nothing new, nothing different, nothing challenging. It doesn't mean they don't have a purpose. They're just not dreaming or believing big enough.

But there's something about you that makes you pick up books like this so you can get a little closer to standing in your purpose and walking in your truth.

Know that the strange looks will happen but don't let those looks throw you off your game. Sometimes you will be alone in your journey. Sometimes you'll even get some dumb questions that might make you a little angry. It's okay. It's common. Just roll with it. This, too shall pass. You have to be willing to get the annoying questions. And, when people don't understand why you do what you do, be willing to let them continue to wonder.

Remember, this is your calling, not theirs. They have their own truths to discover. And whether they choose to ignore or squash their dreams, that's on them. Your journey may be different than the rest. That's okay, too. Just keep walking in and having faith in what you know and watch what happens to your life.

CHAPTER EIGHT

❖❖❖❖❖❖❖❖❖❖

NO MORE SOFT TALK. IT'S MAN-UP *(WOMAN-UP)* TIME!

"Remember, you're not birthing this fire just for yourself, but for many others who need it."

So you've heard a lot of this doom and gloom. Things didn't go well. Bad stuff happened. Negative, negative, negative. Staying in a bad place in your head will never produce positive results for you.

This is where you have to understand that in spite of all of the things that haven't been so unpleasant in your life, you are still a blessed individual. I don't know what your situation is or what your definition of blessed may be, but let's look at it. You're able to read this book with your own eyes. And just in case someone is reading it to you; in case you can't physically see, you can hear the words that are coming from their lips. Do you realize that there are millions of people who can't say the same?

It doesn't matter how many embarrassing, undesirable incidents have happened in your life. There is always a way to turn them into something bright, good, and positive when you use them to serve others. And that, my friend, is where you have to live.

Yes, I've referred to you telling your story, which may not be too sweet in your opinion. The bottom line; you are a blessed individual. Your response to life should become one of gratitude, especially when you're embarking on something major; like this fire you are birthing.

There is something about being able to see the good right in the middle of the bad. If your car gets a flat tire, be grateful that it won't be long before you are up and running again, with another tire, even if it's a rubber donut.

If you got a call from the principal's office because your child has forgotten who they belong to, be glad that you're positioning yourself to be able to stay home and spend time with your child to help him get back on track. And if you're not there yet, be thankful that there are resources that can help you get there.

One thing I've always noticed about successful, happy, helpful people. They hardly ever focus on the negatives. Not that they never acknowledge them, but they always seem to find a way to turn negative situations into something that can become useful and beneficial to others.

Having the right attitude will honestly make the biggest difference in how well you will fare in this birthing process. Giving birth should always be an experience that you look at with high anticipation. I'm speaking of the anticipation of all of the good that will come once the process is complete.

And just like birthing a child, birthing this fire in your belly is also just the beginning. So don't ever start the process with all of the negative, nagging thoughts that you could have. Learn to replace them with positives as quickly as they come.

Yes, there will be those times when your thoughts and feelings are a little less than pleasant. It's a given. Life will see to that. When you find yourself drifting in that direction, you have the responsibility to turn it around. I don't mean for you to become pretentious about what you are dealing with. That's the fake and phony stuff that just doesn't work.

What I mean is, genuinely go to a place in your heart that can help you replace those old thoughts with new thoughts. Successful, happy people do it every day. Sometimes all day. Bad days happen and yes; sometimes you just need to have that time where you let it all out. But you absolutely cannot live there. You MUST turn it around.

Another turn-around you must do...

If you ever find yourself feeling inadequate, doubting yourself and your abilities and wondering if people really want what you have to offer, that's another turn-around that has to happen quickly. Those thoughts will kill your vision faster than the noise of the naysayers.

When you start to play into the doubt that can sometimes creep up, you are setting yourself up for a guaranteed downward spiral, and bouncing back from those thoughts is not always easy. What happens too often is that we go through things and as much as we don't like to admit it, we want other people to feel our pain. We want them to feel sorry for us or throw their arms around us to let us know that everything is going to be alright.

There is absolutely nothing wrong with getting that needed hug or pat on the back telling you that everything is going to be okay, but can I let you in on a little secret? People, for the most part, don't like having to always pick you up if it happens consistently. Yes, they will express their care and concern for you. They will be there for you during those times. But if those times start to happen every time they hear from you, those same people, as much as they love you, will find themselves running in the other direction when they see you coming.

It doesn't mean that they don't care about you and what you're going through, but people are only willing to go so far with you. Why? Because people have their own "stuff" and they really don't want the added pressure of yours, as well.

This is the time and place where you have to learn how to suck it up from time to time. You get to put on your big girl and big boy undies and keep it moving. I know… that may be a little harsh for some, but as I stated at the very beginning, I have to give you what's real. And when you are dealing with other people in any capacity at all, this is a reality that you must grasp.

Most of the time, you can deal with your issues by just walking in your own confidence. And if your faith is weak, do whatever you need to do to build it up. It's necessary for this fire that you're about to birth.

Some of this you will have control over and some you won't. What you can control, do it. What you can't seem to control, get to the bottom of the real issue, fix it and let it go. If you can't change it, ask God for guidance on how to deal with it. Then listen carefully and just follow His lead. And those things that you can change just by changing yourself—

do that, too. Remember, God wants to be in control, but you have to let him.

Sometimes avoiding the downswing comes with just being fully prepared for a task at hand. Sometimes it means practicing something that you could do better so you'll have more confidence when you step out. It's not always bad things that bring on bad feelings. Sometimes it's just those things that make us uncomfortable.

What if you can't "muster up" the gratitude that you need to express?

It happens to the best of us. The first step is knowing that you can't stay in that negative space. The second step is knowing who the person is who without a doubt believes in you and can help you through it.

It's okay to let them know why you're reaching out. This person won't judge you or make you feel worse about the situation that you're in. She always seems to know exactly what to say and when to say it. He somehow always knows what not to say and how to bring a smile to your face. If you have more than one person who fits this bill, all the better, but you only need one. Remember... he's standing with you on that cliff.

Now here's another point. If you don't have people like this in your life, you have to ask yourself why not. Be honest with yourself, then fix it. Every person needs someone in their rah-rah corner. Start figuring out now who sits in that corner for you. I guarantee you will need them at some point. Don't be afraid or ashamed because most likely, in return, you will be that person for someone else.

Here is something I've used many times. I don't

remember where I learned it, but it's called the "as if" mindset. It means that whatever is bringing you down, you start to act "as if" things are just the opposite.

What would you say in that situation? How would you respond? You will act, speak, or do "as if" everything is exactly the way you want it to be. It may not be your reality yet, but first, you have to get your mind right. Eventually, your heart and soul will follow. It points right back to the scripture in Proverbs 23:7 that says, For as he thinks in his heart, so is he.

To me, that's saying that regardless of the circumstances that are currently surrounding you, when you put your mind in the right place your heart will change the way you feel about the matter. In plain English, if you think a better thought you will soon find yourself taking a better action.

What I've found is that the few times I've had to use my own "as if" attitude, it brought me exactly to where I needed to be, even if only to get me through what I needed to do for the moment.

I'll caution you here, too. This is another place where you can't live. "As if" is useful to get you through a moment when you need to be that confident, outgoing YOU. For example, if you had to go on an interview for the job of your life, and something happened earlier in the day that completely threw you off your game, use your "as if" mindset and get that job. But if you need to go back and deal with that issue later, do it. Just don't ever let the issue hinder you from operating at your highest peak, particularly when it matters most.

So, the next time you find yourself becoming a negative Nellie, ask this question. "What is the absolute worst thing that could come out of this?" Now I do realize that in some cases, that worst thing could be devastating and life altering. If your issue is something that you have no control over, use it to build upon the story that you already have.

Remember this. You're birthing this fire, not just for yourself but for many, many people who need it. If your fire gets put out, the world loses. You will have challenges, but it's life. As long as you're on this side of heaven, understand that negative things will happen. But you, my friend, are a warrior, which means you win.

Keep in mind that there are people out there with a problem that only you can help them solve, so you have to stay in man-up/woman-up mode so you can get the job done!

CHAPTER NINE

✦✦✦✦✦✦✦✦✦✦

YOU DO HAVE THE SOLUTION TO SOMEONE'S PROBLEM

"Remember... you could be the light that guides someone to the other side of their dark tunnel."

Now that your head and heart are moving back in the right direction, let's get more practical. When you think about what you are purposed to do, who will it help and who will it bless? Who are you talking to when you deliver your message, offer your service, or sell your product?

In reality, no one person in the world has what absolutely everybody in the world wants or needs. The only person that ever lived that I can think of, who has something that everybody needs is Jesus Christ, Himself. But even with that truth, Christianity is not something that everybody wants. There is no better example.

It's your job to figure out who are the people that want what you have to offer. Not just those who need it. And, you must be careful not to get offended when you discover that even though you have what someone wants or needs, she may not want it from you. Again, don't take it personally. It's not about you. It's about her.

One of the biggest mistakes that a lot of people make, is thinking that because their message is so valuable, that it's for everybody in the world. It may be a message that everyone does need, but if you look around, it won't take long to discover that everyone who needs what you're offering won't bite.

Do you have a message of hope? Great! Hope for what? Hope for who? A person who is addicted to drugs needs hope for deliverance from drugs. This, we know for sure. But remember, back to that "unique" thing. There will be drug counselors who can't emotionally reach every person in need of drug counseling. Here's my example.

If I'd ever been on drugs and needed help, I would have to make a decision. Would I choose someone who has also been on drugs and gotten free or someone who has never been on drugs and can only talk about how to get free? I'd most likely choose to work with the one who has been where I've been, and understands fully what I'm experiencing.

The same would go if someone has a serious illness, and has been told to get their affairs in order. Let's say that he wants to believe for his healing. He would most likely prefer to be helped by someone who is a cancer survivor, than one who has no clue of what it feels like to live through the devastating news of having this illness.

Are you getting my point? Now, I have some pastor

friends who believe that this would never apply to their message. It's because they have a message that could benefit everyone. And, I do get that when it comes to something as important as ones' faith, you can't leave anyone out. I agree—to some extent. At the same time, I can give some examples of how even when it comes to ministry, that some of the most well-known leaders have a specific person in mind when it comes to their delivery style.

I'll go on record saying that yes, the "core" message is one that everyone needs. I will also agree that there is nothing wrong with being specific on who that message is for.

There is one other thing that I believe is important for any leader to know. When you have a message that can benefit people from all walks of life, you will lose many when you try to reach everyone. Let me explain.

Let's start with a brick and mortar business. If you own a hair salon, you want to set up your shop in a way that will attract the clientele that you want to serve. There are some that will pay $200 for a haircut and color while others would squawk at paying $75 for the same service.

Let's say that the $75 stylist can color rings around the $200 stylist. However, when you approach her shop, you see hair all over the floor, signs that are old and outdated, and the stylists are all old enough to be your great-grandmother. (No disrespect to our elders, but there is a point to be made here). It doesn't mean our grandmothers wouldn't or couldn't do a great job. But, if you're looking for the client who is willing to pay $200 for her style, you'd better have a suave looking salon with stylists that look like they know what's happening in today's market.

Now, back to my pastor friends. If you want to build a congregation with people of all ages, you just can't continue serving the same music and programs that our forefathers did. Does it mean that there's anything wrong with your music? Most likely, not. Will you attract those who are not settled in a church already because their grandparents go there? Absolutely not. Whether the reasoning behind this is good or bad doesn't matter. There is a reality that says... I need to see and hear something that I can relate to, yes, even in church.

I understand that those of us in ministry are clear that our message can help everybody. But when we fail to narrow down who it is we're speaking to when it comes to demographics, we often miss the mark. After all, we truly know that everybody needs Jesus, but what we don't like to admit is that everybody doesn't want to hear that message from us because they can't relate to us.

I remember back in my day where all the ladies wore beautiful suits with matching shoes and bags and the hat that looked like it came from outer space. These days, it's a whole different situation. When it comes to certain things, you just have to change with the times.

What people want today is an experience, not a "look" that says I've got it all together. While there are many churches today where the "Sunday-go-to-meeting" attire is still the norm, it's just as normal to see the pastor and leaders in jeans and a button down shirt, which is more relatable to a completely different crowd.

Personally, when I see robes and collars, it gives me an indication of what to expect when I get inside. Again, not meaning it's right or wrong, good or bad. You just usually know what to expect by the "culture" of the people who attend.

Have you ever wondered why so many infomercials about yet another exercise program continue to pop up every month? Have you considered that they ALL make millions of dollars? It bears repeating. It's not just the message that matters. It's also the messenger. People will always have preferences. It's just human nature.

Don't miss the mark by putting the Cart before the horse.

So often as Christians, we want to give people the "come to Jesus" message when they've just lost a child; their house is in foreclosure, or they just got fired and are most concerned about their livelihood.

Don't get me wrong. The people you're speaking to need to hear this message. But again, the Bible teaches me that if I want to win you to Christ, and you haven't eaten for three days, I should offer you a meal first.

In business, I find myself in many circles where people are not into "Churchianity." They often don't know where to turn for real answers. I'm speaking of people with great wealth who you would never expect had any challenges at all. The truth is, many of them are hurting and don't know where to get help or how to cross that bridge or reach that light at the end of their tunnel.

In case you hadn't thought about it, ministry is not always for the downtrodden and homeless and in case I haven't said it already, it's also not always behind a pulpit, holding a microphone, facing 100 pews. And I know I'll catch some flack from my more "traditional" Christian friends for this one, but ministry doesn't always mean opening your Bible and sharing a scripture before you have a conversation or serve someone. It shows up many different ways. That's also another book I may write some day.

Here's what's real. We never move the essence of scripture away from what we do as we walk in our calling, but there are times that we do what we do because of scripture that is alive within us.

If you're in business or ministry, you must know exactly what field in which you should be laboring. You may be called to corporate stages, the mobile store, the school district, or somewhere within the gardening industry. Or perhaps you fit best in one of the seven mountains of influence which are business, education, entertainment, family, government, media, or religion. Just understand clearly what your message is and position yourself so that it can be heard by those who need it most.

The bottom line is, you have a solution to a problem that someone has. Please don't stay pregnant with it forever.

In attempting to carry out your purpose, don't miss the mark. Don't fail to take into consideration the needs of the very people you want to reach. Knowing this will save you so much time in building your community of followers.

If you have a ministry to battered women, let's deal with the matter at hand first. Let's help them find shelter and a place to take their children where they can be safe. Let's lend a listening ear and a shoulder to cry on if needed, before we bash them about being unequally yoked. Hopefully, you wouldn't do that, but I have to throw it in.

People in these situations are aware of the fact that they may have made a wrong decision and have likely heard it all before. You have an important part to play in their lives. Don't miss your opportunity because you're not sure of how or where to start.

So, where do you start?

As you're coming closer to giving birth, my guess is that you probably don't need to look very far to identify the problem and find the solution for those you are called to help with a service or a solution. Here's an exercise that can help you.

Start by making two lists from 1 to 10. On the first list, right down all of the issues that the people you want to reach would have. Example: Let's go back to battered women.

1. They are hurting emotionally
2. They are physically abused
3. They may have self-esteem issues
4. They feel trapped
5. They feel that they have nowhere to turn
6. They live in constant fear
7. They have children
8. They have no help for their children
9. They're lonely
10. They're sad, mad, and sometimes suicidal

Now, this is not my area. However, it took me less than

60 seconds to come up with this list. My point is this. If there is a space in this world that you *are* called to, you should be able to identify the needs of the people in that group quickly, and because you are "assigned" to serve this group, you should have the solutions, as well.

Next, simply write the solution to each issue. If you don't have the solutions, then you know what your first tasks at hand should be. Do some research. Go out and find the answers to their questions.

On your second list, write out ten questions that these women may need an answer to. I won't do it here, but it's very similar to the last exercise. Here, we're not looking for problems; we're looking for questions.

Look at your own purpose; that baby that you're in the process of birthing. Identify who you're going to reach out to and make those two lists. List their concerns and list their questions. Then make a separate list that answers all of them.

Understand that your calling may not be to a group that's having traumatic issues. Your audience may be millionaires who need to know where to put their money for the best tax shelters, or which stocks will give them the best return on their investments. They still have a situation where a solution is needed.

The most important thing to know is who are the people who need to hear the message that you have to share, the product you have to sell, the service that you offer, or the problem that you solve. Now you might be saying to yourself; I don't know the solutions, and I don't have the answers. Your research will be your first step to getting "unstuck" in your own process while you're in labor.

Always keep this in mind. You may be assigned to business, ministry or a cause, but if you don't have answers to the questions that those you're called to serve may have, your purpose for doing the work becomes ineffective and irrelevant.

You have to get this. Even if you aren't personally providing the solutions yourself, find the answers that will direct your group to getting their needs met. People will be drawn to your message because it answers their need. Whether they're having skin break-outs or need to accessorize an outfit, if that's your area of expertise or service, you have the solution to their situation.

Remember what I mentioned earlier. Your purpose may not apply to situations that are problematic or harmful. You may be a travel agent who plans wonderful exotic vacations. Your group still has a need. They don't want to go through the hassle of trying to pull all of the pieces together themselves or where to find the best deals. That's where you come in with the solution to their dilemma.

Your job is to have that "whatever it takes" mentality and get the training and tools you need to be good at what you do. In other words, you have to do your homework. Understand that if your "fire" serves others, it's still ministry. What some believers miss is that our very lives will draw people to our "core" message when we interact with them in the right way.

We will win more when we think, feel, act, and respond the way scripture tells us to. That's called ministering in the marketplace… wherever the marketplace takes you.

CHAPTER TEN

ARE YOU USING THE FAITH FORMULA?

"There is a formula that works for almost every calling that exists. It's time to find yours."

Unless you've attended one of my workshops, you probably have no idea what my **Faith Formula** is. This method is crucial to your delivery process. It lays the foundation and sets the groundwork for everything that's to come and will help you get much clearer on your mission. While we're merely scratching the surface here, you'll still get enough information to help you move forward with your next step.

What exactly is the Faith Formula?

- **Focus** on finding the solution to the biggest question or problem of those you are called to serve.

- **Attract** them to your solution with a compelling message that inspires them to be in action.

- **Inspire** and instill trust so they will stay engaged, connected, and wanting more of what you have to offer.

- **Teach** them what you know with authenticity and honesty so they can easily identify with and relate to you.

- **Help** them to experience your solution through training programs and support.

In the last chapter, we covered the first factor in a little more detail; finding a problem and focusing on solving it.

I spent much more time on the very first factor because it is the foundation upon which every other part of what you do is built. While the other steps are critical, you must get that first step right, or you'll find your journey to be much more challenging.

Now let's move into the other Faith Factors. Remember, we've already reviewed the first one:

1. Focus on finding the solution to the problem.

2. Attract those who need your solution.

I'm sure that you realize that when I speak of attraction here that it has zero to do with an outward appearance. It has everything to do with how those who you're sent to help will find you. Not how will these people find you physically, but will they find you appealing enough to believe that you can respond to the needs they have.

Oh, and I'm not speaking of attracting people through simply closing your eyes and visualizing or sending a picture of what you want out into the universe either. I'm sure that those practices may work for many. Just know that that is not at all what I'm speaking of here.

When I talk about attraction, I mean what will you do, what will you say, and how will you do or say it. How will those that you are trying to reach be drawn to you, over others who offer a similar or the very same solution that you offer? How will you connect with those who need to find you so that they can experience your solution?

Let's start with the most important thing to consider.

Even though you will reach many, always have one specific person in mind. Will she be attracted to you because you speak her language or can relate to her culture or situation? Will he be attracted to you because you have been through some of the things he has been through so he's willing to listen to what you have to say? Will she be attracted to you because as you deal with her, she doesn't feel as though you're judging her? Does he feel safe and at the point where he can trust you, or that you understand exactly where he is in life?

The first step to attracting people to what you have to offer is again, knowing that you won't attract everyone. You'll attract those who need or want what you offer, and who can receive it from YOU in the way that you deliver.

The second step is knowing how they think. You have to consider things like his income bracket, her typical level of education and where they feel most comfortable. You also need to know what would likely push their buttons or push them away. Think long and hard about this one.

What is it about what you have that would make the people you're to serve want to inquire further? Don't feel like you're being too "picky" or particular. You're not. Your job is to narrow down exactly who that person is and center your delivery to suit that individual's need.

In the business world, it's called "target audience." In life, we call it "I know what this person needs and I can help them." This never changes. It's the same in every arena. Whether it's a church, club, or barber shop doesn't matter.

If someone hates opera, they will not be "attracted" to your offer to sell them two tickets to Giulio Cesare by Handel. For some of you, you have no idea of what I'm speaking. So, you would have zero interest in spending your precious time listening to me talk about it or your hard-earned money on tickets to attend. If your main interests are in the area of government, conversation about what's going on in the arts and entertainment arena may be of little interest to you.

You can't miss this point, or it will quietly defeat everything you are attempting to do. Now let's move on to the third factor.

3. Inspire them to connect as you instill trust.

As I've already said, you have to have a solution to this group of people's most pressing needs. Next, you have to attract them to you by being relatable to who they are.

What will cause her to want to stay connected to you? Why would he choose to stay with you instead of continuing to look for someone else who offers the same solution that you have?

Here's another scenario to help you get clarity.

Let's assume that you invited someone to your home for dinner. As you were cooking, you decided to fry an onion on the side. This onion is not part of your recipe, has nothing to do with the meal you're preparing, and won't be served in the food that your guest will receive. The aroma that your guests smelled gave them mouth-watering anticipation, but in reality, there are no onions in the actual meal.

What you actually brought out to serve was a cupcake, which is far from what they smelled or anticipated. Your guest probably won't say anything, but she'll most likely be very disappointed. She'll tell you that she enjoyed your cupcake. But, don't be surprised if she displays no enthusiasm the next time you invite her to dinner.

Why? You attracted her with one thing, but when it came down to what she received, it didn't measure up. You failed miserably in delivering on her expectation. This fire that you're birthing in your belly is very similar.

These days, people can portray themselves in many ways, especially on the internet. A one-man shop can look like a mega corporation. This is not so wrong as long as you're able to deliver on a person's expectation; whether you gave him that expectation or he assumed it doesn't matter.

Ask yourself this question. What am I offering to those that I attract? And once you attract them, ask yourself if they would be happy with what you can actually deliver. Take it a step further—will they want to come back for more? Consider this your glue or "stick-to-itiveness." What is it? Be honest about this or you'll remain foggy to yourself and others.

The truth is, you never want to build up a person's expectation and then disappoint them. I realize that sometimes this is unavoidable because of someone's unrealistic expectation. And when this happens, it's very likely that they won't be inspired enough to come back for more because they'll have an expectation of being let down again.

Your desire to do everything in your power to never disappoint is also why it's so important that you be precise in who you will inspire with what you have to give. This is where so many people get stuck and can't move forward. They see no progress and can't figure out why.

You may know beyond a doubt that you are called to do a thing. But it's the unknown, and the things that you're not sure of or accustomed to that can cause you to freeze up. Don't let that happen.

Consider the fact that I never said this birthing process would be a cakewalk. It will be work but again, so worth it once that fire is out of your belly. Always remember, every person who has done great things in the world started with small beginnings, and so will you. There is nothing wrong with small beginnings and sometimes, this is where you'll learn your biggest lessons.

Also, understand that every great person kept going when it got tough, and so will you. Being clear in your mind on how these things work together is par for the course, and you're on the right track.

So, what's the fourth factor in our Faith Formula?

4. Teach what you truly know.

I've mentioned that you can learn (and teach) from a book or from your personal experience. Here, let's focus on your personal story. A lot can be said about what's going on these days when it comes to leaders, authors, speakers or anyone who has a message and storytelling. You should be aware that so many times, the story doesn't always belong to the person who's sharing it.

This can cause a little confusion but let's get some clarity. Information is information. One plus one will always equal two. It doesn't matter who gives you that information. The message is correct, but the messenger, that's a different story altogether.

Have you ever listened to a person with a beautiful voice sing an inspirational song when they had no connection to the words they were singing? I have. And as beautiful as it can be to the ear, you don't remember it once it's over. It's almost as though they never uttered a sound. It left you clapping and saying "what a beautiful voice," but you don't really remember much about the performance once you leave. The same goes for you. When people can't "feel" you, they will not "hear" you.

Now, have you ever been in a church service where a seasoned little church mother of about 90 years young sang a hymn, and you knew that she knew exactly what those words really meant?

You probably never used the words that spoke about how beautiful her voice may have been, but I can guarantee that your heart was touched, something stirred in your spirit, and a tear or two may have even welled up in your eyes by the time she finished.

That's similar to what happens when it comes to sharing your message. Don't get caught in the trap of speaking just from your head or trying to copy the way some charismatic speaker delivered a message just because it touched you in some way.

Maybe you can get away with that in some arenas. Professors do it all the time, but if you've ever sat in one of those classrooms, you'll remember that those are the classes that you only took because it was part of the curriculum you had to complete; not because of the professor who was teaching.

On the other hand, have you ever wanted to take a class, a course, or listen to a speaker simply because of "who" it was; not even knowing in advance exactly what they would say?

There are a couple of people that I "follow" both in the spiritual and business arena. I buy their products, take their courses and attend their events because I know without a doubt that at the end of the day, they will not disappoint. Being who they are is what makes the difference. Getting back to that broken record; in whatever you do, do YOU. It will work every time, and your "tribe" will stick with you because of it.

There is a saying that so many follow. It's called 'fake it till you make it.' I understand this philosophy and it may work for a minute. However, eventually, your true colors, inabilities or inexperience will be revealed. This is another one of those places where you can't camp out forever.

While "done" is always better than "perfect" you can't wait until you've perfected everything. Do what you can and never try to play copy-cat where a person's heart or life is concerned. You'll fall flat on your face every time. This is serious business, and I hope with everything that's in me, that you will take this to heart. Pray, study, invest and prepare for the work you are called to. Spend time with it. You've got to take people up the mountain, not continuously circling the base.

In other words, if you can't personally relate to the story, leave it for someone else to tell and go and find out what YOU are supposed to share. It will make a world of difference how far you'll go.

I Repeat. Always Share From Your Heart.

Talk about what you are passionate about and where your experiences lie. If you're teaching someone how to make the best barbecue sauce, it should be because you're excited about your own recipe, and you want to share it with the world.

When you are fake and phony, regardless of what you're doing, don't ever think that you're getting away with it. Your pretense speaks loud and clear. It shows up everywhere, and you're not fooling people. Especially not in this day and age. Pretending to be who you are not will cause you to lose followers, clients and credibility faster than you can bat an eye.

Now for the last, but certainly not least factor of our FAITH Formula.

5. Help people experience your solution.

Just help people. It's the most simple, and most profound suggestion that I can give. The Bible talks a lot about giving and receiving. Even individuals who don't read or follow scripture can understand this. You must give out if you want to receive anything in.

So what exactly are you giving? Is it your passion, your gifts, and talents, your message, writings, and talks? What you're giving is you. You're giving whatever that "thing" is—that fire that you've been trying to birth. And when you do, you will be blessed in return, beyond measure.

Now, don't mistake this for meaning that if you're a business owner that you should be doing everything for free or giving everything away and getting no return for it. That's not what I mean at all. Your nature should be, and hopefully is, simply that of a giver.

There's something great that happens for those who don't live their lives with a clenched fist. Clinched fists are afraid to release what they have because of fear, greed or selfishness. People who live this way don't allow space for anything to come in.

One of the best ways to help someone is to train them in something they don't already know. Give them a skill that can help them to elevate their life. You've heard the saying many times. "Give a man a fish and he eats for a day; teach him how to fish and he eats for a lifetime."

I happen to be in ministry, and I also have a business. In my world of business, I give away free clarity sessions to help people discover what their next move should be. In return, I get new "paying" clients all the time. It just works out that way, but it's because of some things that I have put in place when it comes to what I do. You shouldn't always give expecting something in return, but don't let your desire to give put you in financial jeopardy.

Maybe from time to time, you may get that "feeling" that you should offer some service to someone who needs what you have and you know they can't pay you. Do it. It feels amazing! Don't be abused by it, and especially, don't be afraid to be diligent in the part that provides your livelihood.

It is biblical that you receive compensation for the work that you do. It is also biblical that you be a blessing to those in need. Ask for guidance in this area and do what feels right in your spirit. Remember that you are blessed to be a blessing and one who is deserving of pay.

Some things you'll do for free and some you'll do for a fee. Know what this looks like for you and stay within those boundaries. It's not always best to do what "feels" right. Do what "is" right and you'll hit the bulls eye every single time.

CHAPTER ELEVEN

✦✦✦✦✦✦✦✦✦✦

MONEY IS THE ROOT OF ALL EVIL? WHO TOLD YOU THAT LIE?

"Real talk. Money is not evil but answers all things, so don't treat a blessing like it's a curse."

Before we dig any deeper into the fire that you're birthing, I have a question for you. Does what you're birthing have anything to do with making more money or starting a business?

I don't mean to yank you out of that "touchy-feely" place of discovering your purpose and unveiling those things that have held you back. But, I have to talk about this just a little bit because I've discovered something in conversations with people that I coach. Many people can't get to the money part of their passion because somewhere between birth and where they are right now, there is this "sense" that they shouldn't desire wealth because that's somehow wrong.

I'll start this chapter by saying that it was a little uncomfortable for me to write because of where I've come from. One side of my family had a little more wealth than the other. However, both my mom and dad were successful entrepreneurs, and both did well. Even still, there were times in my life where the "money topic" wasn't always positive and in my life, I had to allow God to grow me up in that area so I wouldn't be afraid to have or talk about money because it's part of my calling.

I just wanted to give you a "brace yourself" warning in case you start to squirm a little. I get it. It's okay. You can grow past it like did. That being said...

For many of us, the thought or idea of being wealthy hasn't always been met with positivity—especially if you weren't brought up in a prosperous environment.

Another thing that holds some back from understanding that it's okay to be wealthy is religion. Here is something I'll never understand. Even though we read scripture that tells us that it is good to have abundance—yes, even financial wealth, we aren't receptive to it. We often choose to lean toward the side that says you're more spiritually "in tune" or "connected" (or somehow more holy) if you're okay with never having enough money to pay your bills and have some left over.

I do get it. In a lot of situations the things or should I say the people we've seen that appear to have the most wealth are often not the best examples when it comes to morals and ethics. Why is that? Maybe because it's the way wealthy people are portrayed in Hollywood that leaves us feeling that something is inherently wrong with being rich. Unfortunately, Hollywood doesn't always portray the wealthy in the best light.

But more than likely the reasons are closer to these:

Cultural influencers.

When you were growing up as a child, what was it like culturally for you when it came to money? Were you told that if something cost $4.00 at one store and you could get the same thing for $1.00 at another, that it's better to buy the one for $1.00 even though the quality might be slighter inferior? There's no right or wrong answer here. Just food for thought.

Economic influencers.

Were you told "no" a lot because there wasn't enough money for whatever it was that you wanted? Did you always hear conversations about bills being due but there was never enough money to pay them all? Did your family always worry about not having enough money for almost anything that would come up in conversation?

On the other hand, did you grow up where because of the amount of money you had, there were always happy gatherings, vacations, eating out and shopping often? Keep in mind—the way you grew up around money has the greatest influence on how you perceive being wealthy today. Now, let's move on to the next influencer.

Gender influencers.

Growing up, did you hear that women and men play different roles when it comes to money? For instance, man is the head of the household, therefore, he must be in charge of everything that pertains to finances. Or did you hear... find a man who can take care of you or another one, especially to women; be sure to sock some money away and never depend on a man to take care of you.

It's amazing how people of the same generation can have so many different outlooks. It all depends on how it was in your household.

Geographical origin and influencers.

How was the neighborhood where you grew up? How were the kids in the schools you attended? Were there mansions in your neighborhood or were the homes in disrepair? How did most of the people in the community you lived in view money? Did you experience life where there was not enough to last from paycheck to paycheck or was there an overabundance at the end of the month?

Were there people who thought they were better because they seemed to have more or did they give to those who appeared to have less? Were there those who had low self-esteem because they had less?

What were your feelings about your life as you were growing up in your neighborhood? Again. There is no right or wrong answer here. Just a way for you to reflect on why you may feel the way you do about money.

Spiritual influencers.

Did you ever hear that money was the root of all evil and that somehow if you had a lot of money you weren't a good Christian? Or did you hear that as a Christian, the more you have, the closer you are to God because of all of your blessings?

I know it seems a little strange that there can be so many philosophies from far right to far left and everything in between. But, these influencers have helped to shape all of our thoughts surrounding money.

Before you continue reading, let me forewarn you about the things I'm going to list here. It may be a little harsh for some because of what they've come to believe, but can we get real so we can get unstuck and finally move ahead in this area?

Have you ever considered that your lack of being okay with not having a sufficient cash flow could be linked to any of the points listed below? It's okay if it finds you. It finds many people but now is the time to correct your thinking so you can begin to move forward.

- You're in the "middle-class" so in your opinion; it's all good because you're not in the lower class.

- The people you hang around most don't have money, and you don't want them to be uncomfortable when they're around you.

- You don't want for anything more than you already have, so why strive for more? Just a side note if this is you—what about having enough to be a major blessing to others? Just a thought...

- You want to try something that would bring in more, but you're afraid that you might fail.

- You have the false belief that only highly educated people can have an overflow of income.

- You don't feel that you deserve to have the same wealth that others enjoy.

- You're stuck having to trade time for money, so you don't have time to pursue anything else in your life for pleasure or necessity.

I'm sure you are well aware of this, but I'll say it anyway. The Bible doesn't say that money is the root of all evil. It says that the love of money is the root of all evil. Meaning, some people love money so much that they will do anything, even kill—to get more of it. That's evil to the highest degree.

So what's my whole purpose for writing a chapter like this in the middle of a book that talks about all of the great things surrounding finding and walking in your purpose? It's simple.

What if that fire you're birthing is somehow attached to wealth and riches that await you? It could throw you completely off if your thinking isn't healthy in this area. Whatever you feel about creating wealth and being rich with finances, I want you to understand why you feel the way you do.

I'm not going to say what's good or what's bad, but I will say that according to the Bible "...money answers all things" (Ecclesiastes 10:18-20). In plain English, "money solves problems."

Let's bring it home to what really matters to you most.

For people who like to consider themselves living a moral life and genuinely care about others, there are similar ways to answer this question.

When asked what matters most, people with certain morals will say things like, "I just want to help other people" or "I want to be able to give to XYZ cause or charity so that I can better serve the people with that need." Others might say something like, "I want to help people going through divorce, feed the homeless or help support the children's ministry at my church."

All of these things are relevant and personally, the types of things I believe we should all consider doing. What gets to be perplexing is this. More often than not, the people who want to help the most are those who usually don't have enough. I hope this doesn't come off offensive. That's certainly not my intent, but as I mentioned earlier, this needs to be addressed.

I remember attending events at church where the intentions were to focus on building businesses but being told "this isn't about money... it's about being a blessing to the Kingdom." Okay... I hear you, but I don't get it.

If I want to be a blessing to the Kingdom, can't I do a bit more than just show up and lend a helping hand from time to time? Yes, I will always do that, but if there's a bill that needs to be paid, wouldn't it be better or at least just as good if I'm in a financial position to write a check and pay that bill?

Oh, but, I need to have money to be able to do that. Right? And if I can barely pay my own debt, how could I ever be in a position to help anyone else? So for me to put myself in that position of abundance, don't I need to do something that will allow me to have enough to share?

Unfortunately, too many people are more comfortable with the idea that one day, God is going to pour out blessings from the sky without us having to do anything. Don't get me wrong. I know for a fact that many, many times God will open doors and windows and give us a landslide of blessings that we never saw coming and didn't expect at all. I'm all for that.

However, I do recall in scripture where ten virgins were able to meet the bridegroom because they were prepared with oil for their lamps, while those who had no oil were not allowed in. I also recall where a man gave talents (which literally means money) to his servants to invest. The one who did the most with what he received was awarded more while the one who did nothing with his money had to give up what he had. So, what's my point here?

This fire in your belly may or may not be about anything that has to do with business, wealth or financial gain. However, for some of you, I know for a fact that money does play a part because it constantly comes up in conversation.

If your fire does have to do with business or finances, please don't run away from the idea. Don't be afraid to expect abundance, to be fruitful, to prosper and to multiply. Remember, it's not going to be just about you. Having an abundance is always going to have more to do with those that you'll be able to bless because of it.

To gain a little more clarity of where you stand in

this, ask and answer these questions on why you're going to birth this fire.

What matters most to you?

What is it about this fire that's so important? Is it only about what you can gain for yourself or does it include how you can help someone else?

If you write a list of ten things you'd like to do once you birth this fire, what would those things be? Do any of the things on your list involve money in any way?

Why did you say yes to birthing this fire?

What's behind your reasoning? One thing you'll come to discover is that if this is truly all about money, it won't take you far, and it will never completely be fulfilling. I know for some that may not seem real, but trust me. Whenever anything becomes all about money alone and getting more of it, even after you birth the fire, you still won't be satisfied.

What do you hope to gain, personally, from birthing this fire?

There is always going to be something that is 100% fulfilling for you if you're going in the right direction. Maybe it's to satisfy a hunger for ministry or to fulfill a desire to serve people in a specific way. Maybe it's to start a business and leave a legacy for your family.

I don't want to lose you here, but your fire may not have a spiritual connotation at all. Maybe your joy will come from teaching women how to crochet beautiful sweaters. What you do doesn't matter when it's part of fulfilling the purpose for which you were born. So ask yourself, how will you know when you've reached that place of satisfaction in birthing this fire?

What is your ultimate purpose for birthing this fire?

You must have a crystal clear picture of why you're going to do this. I've already mentioned that at times it will get a little hard, and you'll feel like throwing in the towel. Unless you know 1,000 percent what your "why" is in this endeavor, it will be easy to side-step on your journey or abandon it altogether. Once you know exactly why this has to happen, you're already halfway there.

I sincerely hope that this chapter didn't throw you. I hope that it has simply given you a clearer picture of why you are going to do what you are going to do. My biggest prayer is that you discover that if what you are going to do does have something to do with money, that you won't shy away, and that you will be moral and liberal in how you choose to use it.

CHAPTER TWELVE

❖❖❖❖❖❖❖❖❖❖

LET'S GET CRYSTAL CLEAR ON THE VISION

"It's great to have sight, but understand that sight without vision is a huge disadvantage."

Something amazing happens on the inside when we recognize that there is something big that we are specifically called to do. Sometimes it gives us the chills or maybe goosebumps, particularly in the beginning.

Then as we start to get closer to seeing things take shape, other feelings can creep in. They are the ones that usually keep us from moving forward because we're not certain of what we should be doing to move forward. The main thing to ask yourself is "are you willing."

As long as you desire to move out and give birth to your purpose, your mission, your calling, you will continue to seek answers to the many questions you may have regarding this great mission of yours. I know that feeling, and it's one of the reasons I wrote this book. I had some questions before I started to move forward toward my purpose. The crazier part of this was the fact that I wasn't even sure what those questions were.

I just knew that I had a few unsettling thoughts that made me a little uneasy and unprepared to move forward. My guess is that you may have some of the same questions.

This chapter is intended to help you get real clarity in some areas that are too important to ignore. As you continue to read, I want you not just to make a mental note of some of the things I'll discuss, but it will be helpful for you to write down the answers to some of the questions I'll ask.

Now that you're closer to delivery, I want to give you some important things to consider. It will make a difference in how prepared you are to answer the call. Let's call it your personal plan of action.

Make sure your mindset is in the right place.

One thing you must be clear on is that your purpose may be taking you to a place that you've never been before.

You may find yourself having to think differently now when it comes to making decisions. In the past, you may have considered things the way an employee would and now you have to start thinking like the CEO of a company.

This means that in whatever way you looked at or thought about things as a child, you may need to make a shift. Just like with the way you may have thought about money, how you think about what you do with your life every day may also be slightly different and unfamiliar.

Even if what you're walking into is more about ministry than business, understand that there are not many components that are different, except perhaps your core message. I want you to shift to the mindset that says, if this business, ministry or cause is to be, it is 100% up to me.

I want you to think about the fact that you are the person who must now take the reins and guide this mission to the place it is supposed to be. You won't always have do it alone, and you shouldn't. However, the birthing process is completely on you. This is not a situation where a surrogate can do the job for you.

One of the things that can sometimes get you stuck is wondering if you're really "enough" to bring this thing to pass. Are you good enough, are you smart enough, are you attractive enough, (I know that one threw you, but you'd be surprised.)

Know that you *are* enough. If you weren't, God would not have given this to you. All you need to do now is get clear on some of the questions in your head, and you'll be ready to move forward.

On the next few pages, I'm going to ask you a few questions that I want you to think seriously about to help you gain some clarity. It will be tempting to just read through them and think. But, I'm going to challenge you to actually fill in the blanks. It will make a difference.

Ask and answer these two questions:

1. What is the number one thing holding me back from giving birth to this fire?

   _____
   _____
   _____

2. What is the one thing I can do today that will alleviate whatever is holding me back?

   _____
   _____
   _____

Clarity in your vision will make the difference. Several components make up your vision, which is the big picture. The vision should be what you see at the end. What's the most significant result that will take place when you have accomplished your purpose? Clarity of vision is something you should be seeking the answer to if you don't have it already. Let's start with your purpose.

Remember that island that we talked about in an earlier chapter of this book? That should give you somewhat of a clue of your purpose. What was the thing that you took with you that you'd spend hours doing even if you weren't getting paid for it?

Don't get me wrong, you will and should be well paid for the work you do, but if it all boils down to the money alone, you haven't found your purpose yet.

Ask and answer this question.

What do I believe my purpose is?

_____
_____
_____

The next part of your vision brings into consideration the things that you desire in your heart. I know this might sound very similar to your purpose and your passion, but there is a subtle difference. The desires of your heart are those things that you truly long to see happen for you and others.

The reality of this vision is that thing for which you consistently strive. You can be content with where you are, but you never stop dreaming about those things that are deep in your heart that you want to see come to full fruition.

To see these desires come to pass, you must take action steps; otherwise, they are just dreams that remain stuck in your thoughts. Your desires can come to pass when you do the things that are required to bring them forth. And these desires are usually tied to your purpose.

Ask and answer this question.

What are the biggest desires of my heart?

_____
_____
_____

Now let's think about those things for which you have the most passion. There is something about involving yourself in an activity in such a way that you are the most fulfilled in the process. It could be anything from reading stories to children at the local library to speaking on stages before thousands.

When you are operating within your truest passion, things come easy for you. You feel joy, peace, happiness and you could stay in that space for hours on end. Do you realize that the passion that you have is also God-given and that it helps to guide you right into your purpose?

This is why I tell people all the time; you don't have to be in a pulpit, ordained or licensed to carry out the will of God for your life. You may not even consider what you do to fall into the category of "ministry" but know that anything that you do to serve another person puts you in that arena and may have nothing to do with religion.

Ask and answer this question.

What am I most passionate about?

_____
_____
_____

Are you beginning to get a clearer picture of all of the things that are inside you that will play a major part in your moving out and operating in the area to which you are called? Hopefully, you can answer yes.

This process is all a part of helping you move to the place where you at least know in what direction you should be moving. Now let's take a look at what you do well.

It is sometimes difficult for us to look at ourselves and

know what people would want from us, whether it's in the area of ministry, business or entertainment.

I can recall in one of my coaching sessions where my client was 100% convinced that she had no gifts, no talents, and nothing to offer that would bring anyone to pay her. As we continued to talk, I asked her a few very simple, basic questions.

We discovered that her friends were always coming to her for advice regarding relationships. Whether they were married, single, dating, divorced it didn't matter. There was something about her life experiences that gave her great insight in this area. Even though many times, it was just to comfort someone who just had a bad break-up, she came to the exciting discovery that her gift was to coach people in the areas of love and relationships.

Another client went through something very similar. At our conclusion, he discovered that his gift was training dogs and teaching people how to take better care of the little pooches.

Sometimes our gifts and talents are so close to us; we can't see them. It's now time to dig a little deep to find out what yours might be. Don't mistake this exercise just for the obvious. Even if your gifts are obvious, let's see if there's more.

Is there something that connects with your passion and the desires of your heart that you may have let slip by or is your gift obvious? Are you a great singer, dancer, artist, cook, barber, with the belief that what you do is just a job that pays your bills? Think again. Just like success leaves clues, so do your gifts and talents.

Your gifts come naturally, and your talents can be improved upon with a little time and effort put toward learning and doing. What comes so naturally to you that you hardly have to think about it when you do it? What do you do well, but you'd be great at if you would spend a little time to bring excellence to it?

It's great to be passionate about a thing. Your gifts and talents are also clues to discovering your purpose. When you combine them together, you become an unstoppable force. This is where you become that walking and working in greatness person who shows up in the world exactly as you were intended.

Ask and answer these questions.

What are my gifts?

_____

_____

_____

What are my talents?

_____

_____

_____

Just getting clear in these areas will relax your mind and help you to get a clear focus on where you're heading. Not that you didn't already know but, the clearer the road is, the smoother the journey will be. Though you may be tempted, don't skip answering these questions and actually writing them down. You may have to do some mind-work to complete them, but that's good. The more you dig and discover, the smoother your birthing process.

CHAPTER THIRTEEN

♦♦♦♦♦♦♦♦♦♦

MANAGING THE MANY FACETS OF YOUR NEW LIFE

"When your life begins to change, don't forget to consider the lives of those closest to you."

Now that you're a little more clear on the direction you're heading, you can't ignore what's going on in the rest of your world. Yes, you are called and chosen, but there are other parts of your life that you can't ignore.

I remember when my fire got to the place where it almost felt like I was about to explode. I was incredibly excited about the vision that I'd seen. I knew where I was going, and I was pretty clear on some of the steps I'd need to take to get there. What I wasn't ready for was the possible disruptions that could happen in other parts of my life while I was soaring around on cloud nine.

My immediate family is very small and I must say, they're very comfortable occupying most of my time. To be honest, I wouldn't have it any other way. I was smart enough to know that there was no way that I'd be able to abruptly disrupt my lifestyle without wreaking havoc and bringing confusion to my then normal routine. So, the first order of business was to have a conversation with those closest to me and do my best to explain what was taking place in me.

I explained that there would be times I wouldn't be as available or accessible as I had been, at least for a season. There would be times I would be behind my computer for hours on end. It wouldn't be this way always, but they needed to know that I now have to stick to a "work schedule," and that even though I was doing all of this from home, it was just as important as if I were going to work for someone else at a big corporate office.

I had to hang signs on my door so I wouldn't be disturbed when I was recording a course or having a counseling session over the phone. I had to skip some meals and turn off the television. DVR and I became close friends for the few shows that I do enjoy, but it got to the point where I just didn't have the time even for that. Again... for a season.

My family had to come to the understanding that for now, things won't be as usual.

My next big challenge was decluttering the place where I would work. I'd love to be able to tell you that I succeeded in that one. Well... I did succeed until my mom passed, then all of a sudden the 'order' in my world was temporarily turned upside down.

I will take a quick side-step to say this. When your workspace is cluttered, your mind will also be cluttered. I don't completely understand the relation between a cluttered space manifesting a cluttered mind that ends up in an unorganized business, but I can attest to the fact that it is true. When my workspace is clear, so is my mind, and I get a lot more done with a lot less stress.

In your surroundings, find a place—any place, even if it's the kitchen table or a T.V. tray in the corner of your bedroom, and make it your place to plan and produce. It worked out for me to convert a spare bedroom into an office, but your space doesn't have to be an entire room. As long as your family understands that when you're there, (wherever there is) and it's the time you've put on your schedule to work, you should not be disturbed unless it's an urgent matter that no one else can resolve.

Conquer Your Fears

No doubt you may be walking into unfamiliar territory through this process. It's okay. You're not dealing with more than you can handle.

One thing that keeps many of us stuck in our old ways is fear of the unknown. Remember, God did not give us the spirit of fear, so whatever is causing you to be afraid to step out isn't coming from Him.

One of the best ways to overcome fear is to be well prepared. Whatever it is that you are planning to do, plan to do it with excellence. Spend time building up your confidence by reading, studying or working with a coach or consultant who can help you.

You will also want to be extremely careful about the people with whom you share your vision. I know you may be excited and want to shout from the rooftops. That time will come—believe me. But until it does, be very careful of who you're letting in.

I say this not to make you feel that you need to be secretive about what you're doing, but if you share your vision with the wrong people before the time is right, they will often unintentionally, snuff out your fire with their doubt and unbelief toward what you are doing.

I cannot express this enough. This is YOUR vision. This is YOUR dream and YOUR fire. Don't ever let any outside force, person, or situation cause you to take back-steps. They may have every intention of giving you 'good' advice. But individuals who are not walking in your shoes don't know the mandate that is placed on your life. I've mentioned this before, but now we are dealing with it on a much more practical level.

You may find that you need to stop having certain conversations, stop hanging out with certain friends, and start shutting out the naysayers. It will be hard at first, but you must choose between your success and not hurting someone's feelings. Ouch. I know, but you must do it.

They will understand later. Don't be offensive to those who love and care about you, but you can't let them dump their negativity or unbelief on you. Hearing the wrong words in your ear will have an ill effect on your journey. It can cause you to lose confidence and begin to procrastinate to the point where you won't even understand why things aren't getting done.

Prepare Your "Fire" With Excellence

What are you presenting to the world? For some, it might be a service. Maybe you're a master chef, a fitness coach, or ballet teacher. Or maybe you have a message to share or a movement to start. Maybe you want to build a community of people around a particular need. Whatever it is, people need to see it clearly.

It's very easy to keep whatever you have in mind in your head, but the person who needs it can't benefit if it stays there. You have to know how you are going to present whatever it is that you are offering to the world.

Think about it as delivering a package. Is it an audio or video course? Is it a blog or website with information that a particular group needs to be able to tap into? Is it a congregation that will regularly gather to hear your message? Whatever it is, how will you deliver or package it?

I want you to see your "thing" as an offering... a gift that you are delivering to a very special person. The way you package it matters. The way it looks, tastes, smells; all of it matters. You want it to be aesthetically pleasing to those on the receiving end, even if it's just your words.

As you think about how you are going to present this gift, consider how you feel when you are on the receiving end. Everything in life can be presented in excellence or poor taste. Think about the things you have received that were in poor taste. You probably never wanted to experience it again—at least not from the same place where you had the not-so-good experience.

When you consider your package, think of the absolute best way that you can present it. If it is a physical package that you are providing, decide now on how that package needs to look. If it has sound, figure out where you need to go so that you can produce it with the best quality possible that's within your budget. I know this is another one of those unpopular topics, but it is a real part of your journey and the fire that you are birthing.

If you have ever been to an event that left you feeling that something was missing or something happened there that was undesirable, take note of what it was, how it made you feel and why. Now, as you are preparing to present your event to the world, ensure that you fix the things that were not so good at the event that you didn't enjoy. This goes across the board. I don't know what you're going to present, but I'm certain that whatever it is, there is a way that it can be presented in excellence. We always want to put our best foot forward.

If you want your fire to be prosperous and profitable, consider this. Every single time you step out to do your thing, do your best without fail. Be excellent every time, and if you miss something don't stop or back down. Correct it and keep moving forward.

Invest In Educating Yourself

Do you know everything you need to know to do this right? Do you need legal assistance to set up a non-profit, an LLC or a corporation? Do you need help setting up a website or establishing a professional internet presence? Invest in your education and learn the things that will help you continue to move forward in excellence.

Many things that are incredibly simple become complicated when you don't have a clear understanding of what they are. One mistake that a lot of leaders make is assuming that they can do everything by piecing together little bits of information. I would never tell you that it can't be done that way because many have done it and succeeded.

What I will say is that if you go that route, be prepared to spend a lot of time in trial and error where it doesn't have to be. I don't say this to give you that "negative talk" that instills fear. I say this to encourage you not to try to go it alone if you're not sure about what to do in some areas. And even if you are confident, you still may not be in a position to take on all of the tasks alone. Everyone needs help at some time. Rome was not built in only one day, but also not by only one person.

If I had to do what I've done to launch my purpose all over again, I would have gotten a coach right from the start. Sometimes it's the things that we don't know that we don't know that cause us the most headaches and become the biggest time killers.

What could have been done in 30 days can often take six months when we're trying to figure out what we don't know. I harp on this a bit, not because I'm a coach but because I have come to realize the value of having a coach.

Whatever you are going to launch into the world, there is someone somewhere who has already done it. The people that you see doing something similar to what you're called to do may not be the ones who will show you the ropes. However, it will be well worth your time to spend a little energy discovering who can help you and how they can help you. Just getting out of the gate doesn't have to cost you your life savings. In actuality, you will lose more in revenue if you spend your time making mistakes in areas that you can easily avoid.

Again, I realize that this is not the "feel-good" stuff that we all like to hear about, but it is the necessary thing that will make the difference in whether or not the world will ever experience the fire that you're ready to birth.

You may not be at the place where you are ready to work with a personal coach or consultant. You also may not be in a position to take relevant courses to get you going. At the very least, find someone to which you can be accountable. Even if they are not in the same type of work that you are about to embark upon, choose someone who will hold you to your word.

Let them know what you're doing each week, when a task will be complete and ask them to hold you accountable to it. Having a coach or an accountability partner will take you far in the process of getting out of the gate and on track to realizing your goal.

Plan Your Launch

Out of everything that I have mentioned in this chapter, this is one of the most important. When you make a decision as to when you are going to do this, having a plan in place will put a fire under you that keeps you in action until it's done. Don't just plan in your head. Scripture says in Habakkuk 2:2, that we should "write it down and make it plain" if we want to see it happen.

There is always going to be a system to doing things

properly. For example, there is a date to start your business; there is a date to publish your book, a time to host an event, always a date to DO something. What is the thing that you need to do that shows you have accomplished your first step? Find out what it is and what you need to do to get it accomplished. This phase will require a lot of planning on your part but plan you must. Don't just try to "wing it" in hopes that everything will flow smoothly. You need to put some tools and systems in place to make sure that it's done right.

Here are a few examples.

Most new authors think that writing the content of your book is all you need to do in the beginning stages. Not so. If you're writing a book, don't just think about the content alone. Plan out when you will release it for presale. Decide when you will release it to the general public. On what platforms will you sell it? Who will help you sell it? Are you going to do a book launch and if so, when and where. Who will host it? Will you serve real food or have snacks? Are you getting the picture?

All of these types of decisions need to be made in advance. And this is by no means a full list of every component that's needed. It's just a small example to get your mind ticking about what you may need to be thinking about when it comes to your project.

I strongly suggest that you get out a calendar and a notepad and at least start "brain-dumping" so that you can free your mind to continue the actual development process of launching your gift.

Writing these things down before you're ready to do

them will keep you from trying to work in a place of overwhelm which is no fun at all.

Connect With Your Tribe

Obviously, the fire that you're getting out to the world has to do with other people. Please understand, no matter how it looks in your head or feels in your heart, you don't have a business if you don't have any clients. You don't have a ministry if there aren't any people showing up for you to minister to. You don't have anything to lead if there is nobody following you. Do you get the picture here? Don't be successful just in your head. It takes connecting with real people.

So how do you find your tribe?

You may not want to hear this, but here is the reality. If you want a lot of people to connect with you, you have to market to a lot of people. Now I realize that in some arenas, especially those that are traditionally religious, the idea of marketing almost sounds profane.

It only seems that way because of the way most people perceive marketing. We somehow get the notion that because what we have is so important or profound, that people will just hunt us down to get their hands on it. That couldn't be further from the truth. Do you realize that Jesus Christ, himself was one of the greatest marketers in the world?

He started with just twelve people to spread the word about what He has to offer. Today, you would be hard-pressed to count how many people have now been touched and forever changed by His message.

He could have kept it all to Himself, but Jesus had a complete understanding of the value of what He had to offer—His very life. But, if He and his disciples would never have used the "word-of-mouth" methods available to them at the time, the message of Christ and Christianity would be non-existent today.

So how do we use word of mouth today? Several ways. Starting with having people spread the word to their immediate circles through the Internet, is limitless. When people "share" your content on social media, it's the way of using modern-day word of mouth to get your message out into the marketplace. It's also, unfortunately, another one of those almost "taboo" topics among certain circuits.

You probably won't be surprised to know that it's also another one of those topics that could be a book all by itself. But, there are already tons out there on the subject, so I won't go into significant detail here. Just know that if you are afraid to launch out into the deep where social media is concerned, you absolutely MUST get over it.

Yes, there is a lot of junk and garbage to be found out there, but if those who are deeply entrenched in Satan's kingdom can use it to exploit, slander and bring harmful messages to innocent people, how much more can we use it to shed a message of hope?

And remember, again, this is not limited to those with a faith-based, or self-help message. It can be used to further a business or just about any cause you can imagine.

Don't try to do it all at once. For simplicity sake and to at least get you going, consider starting with the top three social platforms that the demographic of your tribe are using. You will need to do some research to figure this out, but believe me, the time you spend doing so will be well worth it.

Make a Living

So here we are again. Hopefully, by now you don't need to be convinced that you need money. You need it for your family, for your business or ministry and to help others. And if you are of the mindset that you need just enough to make sure you are getting by without lack, stop.

Think about more than your own needs. The money you make is not just intended for how it can build you a bigger barn. Yes, you will do this and more, but if you're not sure on how to feel about it, reflect back on a few chapters ago where we talked about why you feel the way you do.

If you have no problem with the topic of money, you're ready to promote yourself to the next phase, and that is, what will you do to generate the income that is needed. Almost each of these topics could become an entire session within itself.

As a matter of fact, some of the courses that I teach are 100% about some of the topics that I mention here. If you get stuck, you may need to consider taking a couple of these courses to help you move through this process.

It's not difficult to discover the many different ways to monetizing what you do. If you sell a product or offer a service it's a little easier to figure out, but what about you who are entering into ministry? Your purpose and calling are not intended and have never been designed to drain you financially or put you in a position where you are not able to provide the needs of your life and family.

And yes, I do understand very well the whole "God will provide" way of thinking. I don't mean to negate that in any way. There is such a thing as a gift of faith. Just be clear that in His providing, He will often show you avenues and guide you toward opening the right doors for your provision. There are many stories in scripture where God provided, but in most cases, there was still something that a person had to do to receive the provision.

Here's one way to look at it when it comes to ministry. Think of any ministry that you have ever seen on television, especially those connected to a church. Have you ever noticed that the name of the program that comes on television is completely different than the name of the church?

Have you ever noticed that they also provide books, audios, programs, workshops, events, etc., for a small (sometimes not so small) fee? The church, which is often "not-for-profit," is directly related to, but separate from the television show, which is "for profit." The owners of the T.V. station would never say to the ministry, "because this is for God, we're going to give you this air time for free with hopes that you'll give us a donation whenever you're able to." No, it doesn't work that way.

And if your business or ministry is housed in a building that you don't own, you can't tell the owner that instead of paying your lease each month, you can give an offering if you have access at the end of the month. Try that and you'll find yourself on the streets.

There is a business side to every ministry and for Believers, a ministry side to every business. I'll use myself as an example. I am a business owner, and I am also in ministry.

In my business, I provide training and teachings that people purchase. I also offer consultations and programs to help people through different business processes. I'm also a certified life-coach which is very closely related to ministry, but is still under the umbrella of my business. In addition, I have a separate business that works in the area of web design, creating product sales funnels and more. (Yes, I have a very full plate.)

In my ministry, I speak and teach (among many other things). When I speak, I'm sharing the message that God has called me to share and although I am paid to speak, there are times that it does not come with a fee. Do I think ministers should always be paid to speak? No. Do I think it's okay for ministers to be paid to speak? Yes. As I speak, teach, or counsel, whether I'm paid for it or not, I'm still fulfilling my purpose to ultimately share the message of Christ and salvation.

While I am a licensed and ordained minister, my business as a coach, consultant, web designer... is also ministry. I believe that especially for Christians, whatever business you're in, when you do it God's way, it is always ministry. I honestly don't see how you could separate the two. As a Believer, your whole life is ministry, but even more so as you work with and serve others.

I think there is another entire book that I need to write to help you get a full understanding of ministry and business under one umbrella.

We've covered a lot of ground in this chapter. In this fire that you're carrying, you'll no doubt come to realize that there are many components, many facets to the bigger picture.

From family, to career or business, to ministry... While it won't all come at one time, you need clear vision on how to handle each piece. Some pieces you'll get right away. For others, you may need to seek God to give you a better understanding and direction for your next step.

Know that He has called you to serve and He has not called you to live in poverty. If you ask, I know He will make it all plain so you have no confusion of your calling.

This chapter may have put you on pause just for a moment. Maybe you thought you were very close to delivery, but are you certain? Is it really time? Maybe, maybe not. Ever heard of false labor? It happens and it's real.

CHAPTER FOURTEEN

♦♦♦♦♦♦♦♦♦♦♦

OH NO! NOT ANOTHER BRAXTON HICKS

"The mind and body can play tricks on us. Don't push yourself into a premature delivery."

If you've never given birth, you may have no idea what a Braxton Hicks contraction is. Well, let me tell you. It's not fun and feels almost like you're in labor. But then, nothing happens. It's almost like your body is playing tricks on you. How unfair is that—but it happens to women every day.

Your body begins to experience pains that you just *know* have to be it. But wait. Your baby hasn't yet come to full term. So... what's going on? Why is my body telling me that the time is now when I still have so much more time to go? It feels like right now is when this baby is ready to come into the world. Why isn't it happening?

It will be hard for your body and mind to comprehend this phase. You feel like you've been through all of your trimesters, but you're still not full term. You feel like you should be in the delivery room. You actually show up. You're there for a few hours, and the doctor sends you home with nothing more than "it's just not time."

You may be in a place where you feel like you want to scream at the top of your lungs. "This has got to be the time. I know what I'm feeling right now!" But you leave empty handed. Believe it or not, this is one of the phases where you grow the most. It's is where your spiritual birth canal is being stretched, tested and tried. You feel that your body is telling you that it's time to deliver. You have the pains to prove it. You feel your birth canal stretching, and you even feel that you're dilating. But, no results. What's really going on here?

Before you can bring your gift, talent, ability and calling into the world, you have to do many things to prepare. You set up a nursery, you buy the crib, get the diapers and bottles, and you can't even bring the baby home without a car seat.

Sometimes, we want to start pushing for delivery before we are fully prepared. Now the most tricky part of this is when you feel that you've gotten everything in order, but the truth is, there are some things that still need to be developed in the baby, just a little more.

This brings me to the thoughts of being in travail. Exactly what does it mean to be in travail when you're about to birth this fire in your belly? I've experienced it, and it's hard to put in words, but let me try to explain.

Travail is a form of intense prayer of a Spirit-filled Believer connecting to something that grips the heart of God. The person who is in travail is laboring with God for an opening to be created so that whatever is about to be birthed can come forth. It's that intense pain that happens just before a natural baby is born. Before you actually give birth, you're in agony and you may even experience some emotional pain.

To some (in theory) this phase is one of the most beautiful parts of the birthing process. It's very rare that a baby is born without some level of travail. It involves the stretching of your birth canal so that room can be made for your gift, talent, ability, and calling to push through, finally.

As that fire in your belly is finally about to be released, you're not thinking about conception. You're not trying to figure out the how or the why. You're not thinking about the fact that without conception, you could not be giving birth at all. However, you may be wondering why this is all taking so long.

Think about it. You've been carrying this destiny, this purpose, this fire, for a very, very long time. It didn't just start in your teens, last year or nine months ago. It was born with you. It came out of your mother's womb right along with you. However, it had to go through a lot before it would become developed enough for you to bring it forth.

Just as Braxton Hicks feels like it's time for delivery, birthing your vision can sometimes feel like the time is ripe and ready. But be careful. If you push too soon, you could force delivery before the time has fully come.

It's actually sort of funny if you've ever been in a delivery room when the expectant mother is wanting to push, and the nurses are telling her to stop. Really? My body is pushing by itself, and I can't stop it. Yes, it feels right, but the timing is all wrong. You still have to wait a bit longer.

If you push too soon, your baby could be born prematurely, will only suffer and in some cases, may even die. I hate to be so blunt, but I really want you to get this. Your delivery time MUST come to full term before you begin to push.

This is a common season for those who are birthing something great and powerful. You thought it was time to let it all out, but your birth canal hasn't been stretched enough. You didn't realize that there were still some things that needed to be formed in your baby.

You know what else happens during this phase? You'll start to wonder if you're ready. You'd gotten yourself all ready to deliver, but the time wasn't right. And when it didn't happen, you began to doubt. Have you prepared enough? Do you really have what it takes? Maybe I'm not supposed to be doing this. You start to think about all of those times that you mishandled the seasons you've been in. Fear, doubt, and regret try to creep in. After all, there were times before those Braxton Hicks showed up that you felt ready.

Now that you're in travail and the time is close, you're not so sure. Be thankful for this extra time. This time is needed for your baby to continue to develop.

Keep in mind that after your baby is born, you have

to nurture and care for it. You have to nourish it and grow it up. If you would have kept pushing when it wasn't time, you could give birth to an unhealthy, premature baby which would require a lot more work to fully develop.

I can't stress enough how important it is that there is a designated time for your baby to be presented to the world and the last thing you want to do is force it out before its time.

Yes, the seed has been planted, conception has taken place, and there's been some significant development happening in the background. But God is still saying wait.

The time has not yet come. Understand that travail is not a place of comfort. You have to go through all phases before the actual birth can happen.

Conception is not something that can be explained to the fullest by man. Yes, we understand the science of conception, but we don't see what's actually happening on the inside. What we see is a mass that begins to grow and develop. When birth finally happens, we see the destiny and purpose that has been released. God planted the seed in your womb, and you conceived and carried it. Then once it is fully developed, it is ready to be birthed into the world.

Phase 1: You are in pain. It hurts, and you just want the baby out.

Phase 2: You begin to agonize because you don't understand why nothing is happening.

Phase 3: You're having contractions. This time, they're not Braxton Hicks, but you still have a little time.

Phase 4: You begin to dilate, and the stretching of the birth canal starts to happen.

In each of these stages, there is a measuring of how far along you have come with what you have been carrying. It's crucial for you to be clear on which phase of the process you're in.

Here's what you must know. As soon as you conceived, everything was already complete. Because you weren't able to bring it forth and show it to the world right away does not mean that the vision, the mission, the business, did not exist. Remember... the reality is that it was conceived in you before you were born.

Here's an important point I must also make. Please don't make the mistake of trying to force a birth if you have never conceived. That's when you have a psychosomatic pregnancy. Meaning, you thought you were pregnant; your brain tricked your body into thinking you were pregnant and your belly even grew but in reality, there is no real baby. When you have truly been impregnated with dreams, vision, business, ministry, etc., there will be life. There will be a seed that can be nurtured and it won't be just in your imagination.

What's Worse Than Braxton Hicks Contractions? Having to be Induced.

In this chapter, I've touched on a few things. We've talked about the false labor of Braxton Hicks, we've talked about the dangers of pushing before it's time and the misfortune of false pregnancy. What we haven't touched on is what happens when it's your time, and your body refuses to produce the natural reaction of pushing the dream out. That means the expected time of delivery has come and gone, and that fire is still inside your belly.

Now you have to be induced and that's not good.

I have never had this experience and must say that I would never want to. The strange thing about this scenario is that there are times that the pregnancy has not gone full term, but there's a serious need for the baby to come forth right now.

It reminds me of when Scripture tells us that Mary, the mother of Jesus said to him to make wine for the wedding feast. Jesus responded that it was not yet His time. But, you know what happens when a mother speaks. Jesus did what she asked because of the need that was present.

What happens when you find yourself needing to be induced? If that happens, for whatever reason, you now have to be "forced" to deliver. It could also mean that you're overdue (or, you need to be pushed off the cliff.) Your season for delivery came a long time ago, and perhaps travail was too much? Or maybe that fear and doubt that I mentioned before snuck in and paralyzed your vision.

Or just maybe, circumstances around you are calling for your gifts to come forth because there's no one else to step into that space. This is where your baby becomes genius with supernatural growth. However, in most cases, you're the one who says "I'm not quite ready. Can we wait a bit longer?"

Are you aware that sometimes when you don't

deliver at the right time, the pain of delivery will be much worse? I'm not trying to scare you here. I just want you to be aware that just like it's not good to go too soon, it's not good to wait too long.

It doesn't mean that delivery won't happen. You'll just have some extra things that you'll need to work through to bring your vision forth. You cannot stay pregnant forever. Once you have received your marching orders and it's time to deliver, you have nothing more to do than to put yourself in the birthing position.

On the spiritual side of things, you'll know when it's time to deliver if you're "tuned in." You will sometimes get a direct word from God, a prophetic word, an answered prayer or a fulfilled promise.

When it's time to go, you'll feel those first rumblings in your belly. Your water may break, and no one else knows what's going on, but you'll know. You'll know because something in your womb is telling you that the time to give birth is here.

No more Braxton Hicks, no more travailing, no false pregnancies. There's nothing left to do but put yourself in the birthing position and get ready. You've been pregnant with destiny, ministry, movement; it's now about to manifest into the earth realm.

CHAPTER FIFTEEN

◆◆◆◆◆◆◆◆◆◆◆◆

READY FOR THE DELIVERY TABLE

"What comes at the end of a delivery is beautiful. But, just before birth happens... ouch!"

So you've reached the point where you're finally ready to step into the great things that you know for a fact you were put on this earth to do. You've thought about it, you've prayed about it, others have asked you about it. And now it's time for you to move forward and just do it. You know without a doubt that you are destined to do something that will help and bless a lot of people, and you're ready for the challenge. That's a good thing, and your life will be better for it. Good.

Here's one thing that I believe you need to know. If you're a heart-centered entrepreneur, a thought leader, a Christian author, teacher or coach—if you're starting a cause, a group, a ministry or anything that's going to pull people from some form of darkness to a place of light, other forces are working against you. It's a given.

I don't mention this just because I feel this way, but there's a scripture that talks about it. There is a force out there whose whole job is to stop you from walking in your purpose and destiny. Its' job is to put a stop to anything good—anything that will help others do or be better.

Some call it evil forces, some call it karma, and some call it Satan himself. Whoever or whatever you call it, it's the same force. It's an enemy to you stepping out, and it doesn't want to see anything good happen for those who are called according to God's purpose. You may or may not believe it or believe in it. That doesn't alter the facts of its existence.

Not to be coy, but some people don't believe in stopping at red lights. That doesn't prevent them from getting a ticket or having a head-on collision. The fact is, ignorance of the law never changes the law or the consequences that follow.

So here's what I know for certain. If you're among those called by God and destined to do great things, Satan's job is to steal, kill, and destroy everything that you attempt to do that is the will of God. So, if you fall into that category, you know why you've been experiencing such a struggle in birthing your fire. Satan is not your friend.

What else is stopping you?

Now... there is another force that works against us that sometimes has nothing to do with a devil, an evil force or anything else that's outside of ourselves. I know this may be a little "off-putting" for some because we rarely want to see ourselves as the 'culprit' who's keeping us down or holds us back, but sometimes we are our own worst enemy. It's not usually intentional and sometimes we aren't even aware.

I mentioned earlier that we tend to shy away from what we don't understand, or don't know. And, if it's something we've never done before, you can almost forget this being something we'd want to explore further.

After all, why tell me I can be an author when every author that I know of is rich and famous. They're on television, they have radio shows, they own huge businesses and are known by millions of people.

I can't be a teacher. After all, I didn't finish my degree, and everybody knows that without that, I'm not qualified. Who would want to listen to me? Why would they believe me? Where are my credentials? What qualifies me?

And, don't dare tell me that I'm good enough to start a ministry. With all of the dirt I've done? Who me? I got knocked up in my teens, and I wasn't married. And, when I did get married, I didn't stay married. Not the first time... not the second time... not the... who me? Start what? (Oh yes, there are more stories that I could tell. You'll have to come to one of my conferences for that.)

I've lived a lot of life, but... but... but... I'm too fat, I'm too skinny, I'm not pretty (or handsome), I don't have a mansion on a hill... I'm not popular, people laugh at me because I drive an old beat-up jalopy. Let's solve this one right now. Maybe those voices did shed a bit of truth—maybe all truth. So what. I won't tell you to say to those voices that they're filling your head with lies. I'll only say to tell them that none of that matters at all because you have a new truth. Now, let's move on.

You've heard it said, "You can't continue to do the same things and expect different results." I like to put it this way... "You'll never start the next chapter of a book if you keep re-reading the previous one." Life is the same way. You've got to figure out how to get "unstuck" and move to the next chapter. These are facts. If you always turn left at the corner, walk 100 feet and stop, you'll always end up at the same destination. Every time—without fail.

I attended a business seminar years ago, and a very successful woman by the name of Gloria Mayfield Banks made a statement that to this day I've never forgotten.

"Look at your feet." Everybody kept looking at her. Then she said. "Why are you still staring at me? Look at your feet." That's just the way Gloria would communicate. She was hilarious, and I adored her. I wanted to be her... until I learned, I had to be "uniquely" me. Moving on... We all (a little confused) looked our feet (as if we didn't know they were down there). Then she said, "If you keep doing what you've been doing for the last five years, your feet are going to be in the same spot five years from now."

Now, that may not be very profound for you. But there was something about not just what she said but more so, the way she said it that struck a chord and made a significant impact on my life. It changed the way I would conduct my business, establish my goals, and even plan my daily activities from that point on. Yes, I finally got it. I realized that day that I'd been wishing and hoping for something specific, something better, something that I really did believe in, but I'd never taken the necessary steps (I never moved my feet), or did anything that would manifest a different outcome. That's why I had been stuck for so long.

This is the point in my life where I started to become a sponge. I wanted to learn everything I could about being successful in what I was attempting to do.

I believe the same goes for where you are on the delivery table. You HAVE to DO something different if you want to SEE something different. There's just no other way around it. I believe you've started the process by not just picking up, but by reading this book. In it, you've gotten a few tips on basic principles of starting any endeavor, especially those that involve other people. You'll be able to get it right from the very beginning.

Here's a clue. Whether you're writing a book, creating a blog or podcast, starting a group or ministry, conducting a webinar or giving a speech, you have to have passion, the right skillset, and the right mindset. Passion will keep you working when you don't feel like it. Having the skills will help you get it done when there's no one around to help you. The right mindset will put you on the right path from the start and save you hours and hours of wasted time, money and frustration.

You've heard it said—"What you don't know can't hurt you." The reality is "What you don't know can kill you," or in this case, kill your vision, keep you from your purpose and cause you to miss your mark completely.

At this point, you should have some insight on some of the things you need first to believe, understand, then do. It's now time to start pushing.

This part may not be a lot of fun for you either, but it would be wrong of me not to forewarn you of what to expect.

You're on the delivery table now. In your body and mind,

you've been experiencing everything that goes along with carrying this fire. You've come a long way, and you know that pushing that baby back in is not and will never be an option. Not only is it not an option, but it's also impossible to do. So, you have no choice but to go through the labor and keep pushing until you give birth. Trust me. When it's all said and done, it will all be well worth it.

I also know that good or bad, life always happens which is probably one of the reasons you HAVE to birth this baby; your ministry, your business, your book, your dream, this fire in your belly. Why? As life is happening for you, it's also happening for other people—at this very moment. It bears repeating that what you're about to deliver could be the very thing that bridges the gap between someone else's pain and possibility.

And as you are probably already aware, the hardest part of the delivery always comes just before that final push. Your body knows that something amazing is on the horizon, and as amazing as it is, you go through just about every emotion possible, right there on that delivery table.

You get angry, you get scared, you want to squash the pain of delivery, so you seek pain relievers, and you want them NOW; not tomorrow, not next week, but right now. In real life, we display these feelings by, pulling down the shades and staying in bed all day. Or we'll just do everything possible to keep ourselves occupied. Let's get so busy that we drown out that nagging, birthing thing that's trying to take place right now.

Honestly speaking and I hate to say it but, this is where you start to regret that you ever got pregnant with this "great mission" in the first place. And dare I say... if you could, you might even consider aborting, even at this late stage. I know that fear, too. Now your head will start to fill up with doubt and disappointment when there really isn't anything to be disappointed about.

I'm also familiar with that head chatter... "Why did God pick me? I don't know if I can do this. What if I'm not good at it? What if nobody wants it? Do I know enough?" Right. What if nobody wants to read what you write, hear your song, eat your cooking or let you even come close to cutting their hair or baby-sitting their kids? If you're honest, you probably know what some of that chatter sounds like, too.

You'll very likely try not think those thoughts because you've been told that only weak people think that way. What you also may not know is that these same thoughts often play out in ways where you don't even realize what's happening.

Your already busy life becomes so much more hectic that you have to push your delivery date to the back burner. Of course, not because you want to; you HAVE to because this other stuff just has to get done first. Of course, it does. "I'll come back to the delivery table when it's more convenient." Can I let you in on a little secret? There will never be a perfect time. Just thought you might want to know that.

Then there's that point where you start to experience that quiet fear. It's quiet because if it were in your face, you'd recognize it and defeat it quickly. Silent fear is much more dangerous because, in actuality, it jumps up to bite you and then shuts you down before you ever realize what happened. It camouflages itself to the point that you become afraid of failure, you're scared of success, you're afraid of the unknown, or you're fearful of what you do know for sure.

In every scenario, it will cause your actions to freeze up,

get stuck or, it will cause you to get too busy to get anything accomplished. So, what do you do when all of this starts to happen?

You're already in mid-delivery, and you can't stop the push. Your only choice? Squint your eyes, grit your teeth and push with everything in your heart. This is where you have to quiet the pain that the body is experiencing, (or in this case, your emotions) and let the heart and spirit take full control.

CHAPTER SIXTEEN

◆◆◆◆◆◆◆◆◆◆

LET'S GO FOR THE FINAL PUSH

"Now is the time to bare down. Let's make that final push with everything you've got."

Let me give you a gentle reminder now. Know that your heart always knows what to do. Sometimes your spirit can be a little wounded, but it still knows what's right; if it's properly connected to God. When all of this doubt and all of the interruptions have halted your progress, it's time to get back up and dust yourself off and make a determination that you will have this baby no matter what. This fire that's been burning in you for years MUST be released! This is where you realize that you refuse to let your past wounds have an effect on your present womb. Start by taking baby steps. If you've been crawling, start to walk. If you've been walking, start to run. If running, leap over that hurdle and keep moving forward.

Understand that every race can be finished. So what if you didn't cross the line in the first spot. So what if you didn't look cute in the process of running. Maybe you caught a cramp in your leg or fell and busted your lip or bruised your arm. What's important is that you get up, you keep running, (or in our case, you keep pushing) until you finish.

Don't let what others don't believe about your vision change what YOU believe about it. I have to say it again. This vision... this fire... wasn't given to them. It has been given to you. It wasn't planted in the soul of "those people." It was planted in yours. That means that what someone else does or does not do, what he says or she does not say, how "they" cheer you on (or not), can have no bearing on your outcome.

Please hear me very clearly. YOU have a message that without being heard, would be devastating to those who are waiting to hear it. You have been given a way to serve people that will change their lives and that, you can't ignore. What you are carrying was placed inside of you because you have the capacity to stand, even through the tough times, and not quit or give up in the middle of the journey.

Realize that when God chose you for this, He did not make any mistakes or change His mind in mid-stream. He knew exactly who you were before your conception was ever thought of by your parents. Even before their conception was thought of. And if we want to go deep, He knew who you were before he created Adam and Eve and that He could trust you with this fire, this vision, before you ever saw it or thought it possible.

I know... it seems too big sometimes. God knew that it would be. He also knows that you can handle it and that there would come a time where you would be afraid to let your bright light shine because you feel that you need to diminish who you are so that you don't come across too bright or what some may call "being prideful." Don't fall into that trap where you want certain others to shine brighter in your presence just because "as things go," that's the proper protocol. Come out of religion and get back to relationship. Remember... it's not your light. It's HIS!! So I say... shine on!!!

Never dim your light to make another person feel comfortable!

Consider that the light of your fire may encourage someone else to want to step up. Walk in your greatness and walk in YOUR truth. Give those who have issues with your bright light a pair of sunglasses and you keep shining. Their eyes will soon adjust. And if not, it's not your responsibility. YOU just keep shining brightly.

And in case you aren't crystal clear, it doesn't matter what has happened in your past. Those mess ups, they all served a purpose. No, it wasn't intended for you to go through hurt or pain just because. However, those messes have now become your message, and what a message it is. And those hard times that you've endured, those crazy things that you've defeated, all of those life challenges that you have conquered, don't despise them. Use them to illuminate your light. Remember, you are no longer the victim. You are walking in victory, and your "win" needs to be seen and heard by everyone you come in contact with. You just have to be willing to lay it all out there. Tell your story. Share your journey, and let people see that the greater one who lives in you has brought you through all of that and formed you to become the person you are today.

Use the past to let others know that as hard as it gets; there is a light at the end of the tunnel. They may not be able to see it for themselves right now, but what if YOU are the person who's supposed to lead them through the tunnel and to that light. If you stay hidden, we can't see you. If you don't write, if you don't speak, if you don't teach we can't hear you.

If your dream dies, your vision is squashed, and your fire doesn't just go dim, it gets snuffed out completely. Those that you were sent to help may now never get through their tunnel—forget about reaching that light at the end of it. And don't think that if your dream does not have anything to do with ministry or helping people with life issues that this doesn't apply to you, or that your purpose is less important. Whatever your purpose may be, it's needed by somebody (actually, a lot of somebodies).

I remember having a conversation with a friend a few years back. Every time she would see a sanitation worker, she would always refer to them as being at the bottom of the heap. She would say things like "I sure hope that guy she's dating is not a garbage man..." with a little giggle; implying that if he was, he was less than desirable.

The last time she said that I asked her a very simple, but in my opinion, necessary question. "Have you ever thought about how this world would be if our garbage never got picked up? Better yet, if your trash cans were overflowing, who would you be happiest to see?" She never made those remarks again.

So whatever it is that you're birthing, never look at it as being any less important than what that person you admire most has done. Know that what you do is needed by somebody every single day. It's true. What you do or say can cause somebody, somewhere to have a very, very good day. Understand that you were born to be a blessing to a specific group of people in the world.

I'll say this again. You may have a ministry, mission, movement, business, book, cause, or message inside of you. If it doesn't get delivered, the world will be short changed. I need you and the world needs you. Never underestimate the greatness that is in you. The purpose is not to cause you to be puffed up, but to cause someone else's life to be changed because of who and what's inside you.

Think back on that ice cube that I mentioned earlier. It started off as water, representing your spirit that flows freely. When it gets cold, it freezes and only becomes useful again as it starts to melt in whatever liquid that surrounds it.

If you have found yourself allowing your dream to freeze up like that cube of ice, it's time to thaw it out, so it can begin to flow and effect change for the rest of us.

If you're on that delivery table, it's time to give that final push. We're waiting for you to push. We need you to push. We're cheering you on as you push. It's okay to squeeze our hands and scream as you push. We get it and we know you can do it. Push through the doubt, push through the fear and push through the head chatter.

This is where you start to look for the baby's crown.

Keep pushing until you see it. That's usually when the midwife yells "it's crowning." That's the sign that the opening of the birth canal has expanded enough to accommodate the dream, the vision, the purpose, and destiny that you're about to birth into the earth realm.

Keep pushing. Right now is not the time to get distracted or exhausted. This isn't when you quit or throw in the towel. It's too late. Now is when God begins to give you that supernatural second wind; that one last push that will enable you to finally deliver. It comes out of nowhere. Just when you're on the verge of giving up, help comes like a midwife.

You're not laboring by yourself. God is right with you. He partners with you as you go into travail. You have no vocabulary because the pain is intense. You just groan. It's ok to groan. What you're birthing at this very moment is seeking its' time and space.

After you've made that final push, what's the reward? How about happiness, fulfillment, peace, contentment; I could go on, but you get the picture. All of those experiences will be so worth all the "stuff" you had to push through to finally birth this fire. There are no words that can describe the pure joy and satisfaction that you will experience once you have delivered.

And when that fire is finally ready to be released in the earth realm, it will continue to burn, but not inside your belly. That discomfort that was once in the pit of your stomach will cease. That feeling of dissatisfaction will be satisfied. That antsy uneasiness will become a place of calm delight. It's what happens after birth.

In all of that agony from the pain of delivery, you're about to have the biggest smile on your face. That's okay; it's normal. If you're a mother and have ever delivered a baby, you know that feeling. If you're a father who has been in the delivery room as your baby was being born, you've seen the expressions of that feeling.

As soon as the baby slips through the birth canal that has been stretched and possibly a little ripped and torn, you completely forget about the pain that was there just moments before. All of your focus has now turned to that beautiful little bundle all snuggled in your arms. The baby is out, and now life begins. So it is for you.

That enemy that tried so hard to keep your fire in has lost the battle. He thought he could make your time of travail so difficult that you would want to stop pushing and persisting, but you didn't stop. Your moment of truth has arrived, you've given birth to destiny and purpose, and you are now in your new season.

Your brilliance is ready to shine all over the world. Not for every person, but to those for which you've been given that special assignment. They don't know it yet, but one day they will thank you for persevering and pushing through. They'll appreciate you for being strong, resilient, persistent and not quitting.

You had no doubt that there was something in you that needed to reach for something greater. It wasn't about the rat race and it wasn't about the expectations of others. It was about that fire within that has been burning and waiting to be released since before your conception.

It's Time to Celebrate your Victory

What a time of celebration. The world is waiting to see your beautiful baby. You should be bursting with joy and you should be Godly proud that you did it. Know that God's got your back. You should celebrate now because you're no longer confused and in the dark about finally walking and working in your truth. You have moved away from the state of not knowing what to do with that burning fire to seeing its' radiance and beauty right before your eyes.

You are ready to pour into the lives of others. You know that the solution, service, or message that you've been carrying for so long is ready for you to share with those who are waiting for it. You can now fulfill your purpose, enjoy your passion and do it all while having the provision for everything you need.

How will you celebrate? For starters, thank God for giving you the strength to finally push and deliver. Then go and do something for yourself that you've been sliding to the back-burner for too long. Even if it's something as simple as going to the grocery store and picking up a pint of your favorite ice cream or flavored popcorn, put it with that movie that you've been too busy to watch and, wallah!

Next, contact all of the people who helped you. Call your midwife and all those who had a hand in the process of you making this final push. Maybe they prayed for you, helped you administratively, monetarily, or just lent a listening ear when you needed it. Take them out to dinner or have a party in your home. Do something to show your gratitude.

Celebrate the fact that you have finally given birth to

that fire in your belly. Make this a standard practice as you continue to move forward in experience and bite-sized successes. Always celebrate the milestones as your fire continues to burn, no matter how bright or small the flame. Keep in mind that this is just the beginning. Enjoy these early days and years, smile at the accomplishments as your fire continues to burn. Keep fanning the flame and be happy that you can say that this was a job well done.

CHAPTER SEVENTEEN

♦♦♦♦♦♦♦♦♦♦♦

YOU'VE GOTTA KEEP FANNING THE FLAME

"A fire can easily go out if it's not tended to. Keep fanning the flame so it continues to burn."

So here we are. The baby is out and it's time to present her to the world. We are all amazed at her beauty. Your fire is burning so brightly that it's leading the way for many. I'm so happy for you.

When I first set out to write this book, my intention was to stay very generic so that even a non-Christian would be able to understand and relate. Well, I think that got squashed early on, so I might as well go all in. I also realize that for those who pick up books and read the last chapter before they decide if they want to dive all in, this could be a "turn-off." I'm well aware of this. And even though I believe the words in this book can apply to people of many walks of life, if this chapter disturbs you in any way, you may be a little uncomfortable with the rest of the book. I just thought it fair to give you fore-warning.

The first thing I want you to think about is a very natural process. It's one thing to do all of the pre-preparation when we're about to bring a new baby home. As mentioned earlier, we get the nursery ready, buy a crib, bassinette, the car seat and all of the things that a newborn needs before arriving home. What we haven't touched on is all of the nurturing that the baby needs once she gets here.

What does a mother do when she brings a newborn baby home? She makes sure that he's fed regularly, his diapers are changed so that he doesn't develop diaper rash, she ensures that her baby gets the necessary naps, and is never exposed to dangerous elements so that he can stay healthy.

Many mothers even go the extra mile of not allowing anyone but immediate family members around the baby for a season. After all, who wants outside germs and all the other possibilities of uncleanness that a newborn hasn't built up enough immunity to guard against. I don't blame new mothers who do this, and I totally get it. I was that way with my daughter.

So, let's talk about this fire that you've just delivered. The birthing of your fire is a natural thing, but for a Believer, it's also a Spiritual matter. Your fire has to be nurtured, cared for, and protected much like a newborn baby. Now that your fire is exposed to the elements, let's take extra precaution to keep your flame burning.

In the natural, you will continue to feed and nurture your fire through staying aware of the needs of those it is burning for. You will stay connected to the pulse of what is happen within your industry by keeping your ears and eyes open. You won't get so comfortable that you let the flames get dim or completely burn because they didn't have enough oil to keep burning.

You'll attend events, seminars, workshops, get coaching and anything else that's needed to keep you at the forefront of your game. You never want to neglect the importance of investing in information that is helpful to keep you growing.

You won't compare yourself to the next person who's doing something similar to what you do. Your main concern is continuing to be authentic in all that you do, not copy-catting anyone else.

You'll continue to thrive and grow and add any additional components that become necessary to not only maintain but to continue growing in every area possible.

All of these things are pretty simple and almost status quo in the world of visionaries and people who have taken it upon themselves to step outside the box and become extraordinary. However, there is another very important component that I would be remise to ignore.

Just like I gave you some tips and steps to follow on the natural side of things early on, I want to give you a quick tip on how to continue fanning your flame.

Whether or not this applies to you, I don't know. Let me explain. You are going to keep your fire burning and take care of your baby not just by what you do in the natural , but by what you do in the spiritual realm. Here is the key.

For our purposes, the nurturing of this baby comes with your understanding of the importance of prayer. If you're a praying woman or man, I will assume that your initial prayer was answered once you gave birth to your vision. Now we are going to make the right declaration that you will continue to take good care of your baby by continuing to walk in the victory you have just stepped into.

Here's an important key. If God is in you, victory is already yours. In our view, the win is not just the birthing of your fire, but the continuance of your flame and the true declaration that it will never go out. But there is something you must do. You must continue to fan the flame.

So when situations arise that try to manipulate, intimidate, or bribe you to snuff your fire, don't let it happen. Know that no matter what it starts to look like as your baby continues to grow and develop, you are already walking in victory.

If you don't see that victory with your natural eye, realize that it begins in the spirit and remains whether you see it or not. Never let your surrounding circumstances deceive you. Even if everything looks perfect, don't get lazy or too comfortable. Keep fanning your flame.

So I have a very important question that you really must have the answer to.

Do you have a clear understanding of what you have just done?

Do you know what birthing your fire is really all about? Make sure that you are clear because when you have an unclouded understanding of it all, your fire will be outstanding. Scripture says that in all of your getting, get an understanding. Think about it, ponder it, pray about it and get clear.

When you are clear, you will be able to declare and command that your fire goes where it's supposed to go and that it burns where it's supposed to burn. In plain talk, let's make sure that you're doing everything within God's power and your willingness to work that will properly nurture this fire you have been given.

When I say you need to pray, I don't mean just any prayer, I mean a prayer that decrees and commands that God's will continue to be made manifest within your fire. I am going to try my best not to go too deep where it starts to get confusing, but stick with me. I'm sure you'll get it.

Scripture says in Job 22:28 that if you decree a thing, it will be established for you. Simply put, if you command it and it's within God's will, it will be done for you. You simply have to know what God's will is. Now this goes far beyond just what you say out of your mouth. It's a heart matter combined with a Spirit matter that makes all the difference. It would take a lot of teaching to break all of this down, but for those who get it, please don't forget it.

With a heart and a spirit in the right place, the words you speak carry power. According to Job 22:28, when you decree a thing, it will come to pass. You have to know this and believe it without wavering—and it has to be connected to the right Spirit (capital S). That's why you must have clarity about the fire you have birthed.

If you're not clear, you won't know what to decree. Understand also that it is up to you to do the decreeing. That doesn't mean that you can't have others to stand in agreement with you. By all means, find those who will intercede on your behalf.

Also keep in mind that just like this fire was YOUR vision and YOUR purpose, the continued work is yours to do, as well. YOU have the authority given by God to use your mouth to keep your fire burning. If God had something to do with your fire being birthed, you can rest assured that the flame will stay lit if you continue to fan it.

Prayer is important to keep your foundation strong. Just like a building; if the foundation is built on sand, it will not stand. By the same token, a new building can't be built on top of a weak foundation that is crushed and crumbling. When a foundation is faulty, it must be completely demolished and rebuilt before anything can be erected on it. Otherwise, the new structure will soon crumble, as well. Simply put, if your foundation is already strong, great. If it is cracked and crumbling, you cannot erect anything new on top of it.

Here's the good news. You just gave birth. Now might be a good time to rebuild the foundation from which your fire will burn. For me, that foundation is Jesus. Yours may be different and you certainly have the right and privilege to believe as you choose. I choose to believe that my foundation allows me to build my fire upon a foundation that is solid, undefiled, and pure.

As I was halfway through writing this book, I was given a few words that I believe came directly from the heart of God. In my first draft, I interrupted what I'd been writing to write the words I heard. Looking at it in its natural flow, it didn't make sense to put it where I had paused in my writing.

In the third draft, I took it out completely because as an editor would probably put it, it just didn't make sense in the scope of what I had written in that chapter.

However, I've come to learn that a lot of what God does doesn't make natural sense to us because He is a Spirit and sometimes things of the spirit don't always seem to flow with things in the natural, even though the Spirit never makes mistakes. What I do know is how to hear God's voice and on my final draft, He told me to put those words back in this book. I wasn't sure where, but that doesn't matter now.

You may not get it, which means these words may not be for you, specifically... at least not right now. But someone, somewhere will read these words and it will be exactly what they needed to hear right now.

It is for you (whoever you are) that I include the following... from God's heart to yours.

"I am God who loves you and does not judge you. You have been disillusioned by what you've seen and heard in many churches that are open in my name. I'm calling you back to me... not for the sake of religion, but because I want you to be back in relationship with me. When you come back to me, you will be amazed at how you'll begin to desire more of what I want for your life and less of

what you thought you wanted. It's not about the do's and don'ts or the people that tainted my name that eventually drew you away as much as it is about your relationship with me. As you draw closer to me again, the do's and don'ts will take care of themselves. Don't worry about those things now. See yourself as I see you. Just stay focused on getting back to me, the one who never stopped loving you, wants to heal, help, and deliver you. I never stopped loving you, so please come home again."

I know this little side journey isn't for everyone who reads this book. It may even be offensive to some. If this wasn't for you, it's okay. Don't forget the rest of the book because this may have thrown you. But if it was intended for just one person who reads this book, then it was worth me going against the grain to obey His desire for you. So now, here's the part I'll add. If you're the one God was reaching out to and you're ready to come back, simply pray this very short prayer and mean it in your heart and you've already taken the first step.

"Dear God, I believe that your son, Jesus Christ, died for my sins, was resurrected from the dead, is alive, and hears my prayer. I invite Jesus to become the Lord of my life and to rule and reign in my heart from this day forward. Please send your Holy Spirit to help me do Your will for the rest of my life. I pray this prayer with belief in my heart that you hear me, in Jesus name. Amen."

Well, there it is. I pray that this book has found you somewhere within these pages. Whether you needed to birth a fire, rekindle a fire, or get to the very end so you could rekindle your relationship with God, it has served its purpose.

If you found yourself giving birth, I thank you, your followers thank you, and that fire in your belly thanks you the most. When you've followed the simple promptings in this book, and prayed diligently for direction of your next best move, you will have finally pushed and delivered your purpose into the world.

Jeremiah 29:11 says "For I know the plans I have for you declares the Lord, "plans to prosper you and not to harm you, plans to give you hope and a future."

It is my belief that your future is bright and the birthing of your fire will make it even brighter. I literally pray for every person who reads this book, so know that someone else is in your corner cheering you on and praying for you every day.

Always remember that you are unique and no one else can do what you do in the way that you do it. Remember that God created you with a specific purpose in mind. That purpose will remain with you always, whether you walk in it or not, so you may as well do it.

The power is in your hands to will and to do what you should. Don't give that will away and don't let anyone snatch it from you.

Remember that you were created in God's image. What you do in life is a direct reflection of who He is in you, and His reflection is always bright.

As you birth this fire and step into your purpose I pray that you will always radiate the very nature of the God who created you.

Never forget who you are in Him and who He is in

you. Understand that your purpose and calling will never disappear but will only grow stronger as you continue to seek His will.

I pray that this book has been an encouragement to you and those who will experience your fire; and that God's blessings will be upon you as you continue to move forward in His name!!

READY FOR YOUR NEXT STEP?

Join the Birthing the Fire Challenge

www.birthingthefirechallenge.com

Even though you know you have a fire burning in your belly, it takes courage to finally do something about it. You have to be bold, fearless, and full of faith to take the very first step. It's one thing to know what's going on – it's another thing to know what steps to take to actually do something about it.

If you're ready to step into your purpose and start creating change right now join the challenge then...

JOIN THE FACEBOOK GROUP!

www.birthingthefiregroup.com

Join a group of like-minded individuals who can't wait to cheer you on. When you join the challenge and the Facebook group, you'll gain access to many more useful tools and resources that will keep you walking down your path of destiny and on track to living your purpose.

ABOUT THE AUTHOR

Rosalind Green knew from her elementary school years that she would be a teacher. Her first thought was that she would teach in the traditional school district in her local hometown, but as life would unfold those plans would come to a screeching halt.

In her corporate career, she managed a department of Judicial Assistants in multiple counties of the Superior Court system of the State of California. It would be there that she would realize that the corporate world was not her destiny. She took early retirement to pursue entrepreneurship and has never looked back.

Her early years of owning her own business started with direct sales where she would walk stages, win cars and prizes and plan and sponsor corporate events for a company of tens of thousands of representatives.

While Ros enjoyed the excitement surrounding this

industry, once again, she came to realize that it was simply a temporary means to an end and a stepping stone to the leadership that would be required as she moved deeper into her purpose.

A Published Author, Transformational Speaker, Licensed and Ordained Minister, Certified Life and Business Coach, and the CEO of Faith and Works 360, Ros has come to value the importance of discovering your purpose, getting clarity in your calling and showing up in the world exactly the way God intended.

She believes that every Believer of Jesus Christ is called to reach a particular group of people through their gifts, talents, business and ministry. Ros has lived through many twists and turns throughout the earlier years of her life. *"I like to look at some of the messes that I've experienced as an opportunity to share a message that can impact the lives of others."*

Ros is unafraid to bring the raw truth with pure authenticity at her workshops and events. She reaches out to those in business who are "called" to what they do to operate from a place of service. She also relates clearly to those who are called to ministry with a desire to blend their livelihood with the spiritual calling on their lives.

Her workshops are exciting and life-changing and not designed for hype. They provide training and guidance on how to be "on purpose" in getting that first book written, that message delivered, or that course or coaching business established.

To find out more about Rosalind Green visit:

www.rosgreen.com